D0871533

In Commemoration
of
The Seventieth Anniversary
of Introduction of
Buddhism to U.S.A.

THE TEACHING

OF

BUDDHA

A Compendium of
Many Scriptures Translated
from the Japanese

References :
American Buddhist Academy
331 Riverside Drive,
New York 25, N.Y.
Tri-State Buddhist Church
1947 Lawrence St.,
Denver 2, Colorado, U.S.A.
Bukkyo Dendo Kyokai
Mitutoyo Mfg. Co., Ltd.
c/o Tokuei-Bldg.
No. 7, 33, 5-chome,
Shiba, Minato-Ku, Tokyo
Telephone, Key No. 453-3331

Printed by Kenkyusha Printing Co.
Tokyo, Japan

CONTENTS

Chapter Two   Practical Guide To True Living.

Chapter Three   Building a Buddha-Land.

The Appendix

PREFACE

In the summer of this year there was held, under the auspices of the Federation of All Young Buddhist Associations of Japan, the Second General Conference of the Pan-Pacific Young Buddhist Associations, which was honoured by the presence of a large number of youthful adherents to the religion, as well as distinguished prelates and laymen, gathered together from a wide variety of countries and climes.

While presenting the spectacle of an international assembly so far without precedent in the history of the Buddhist religion of our country, the present Conference has offered the most indisputable and convincing evidence of its being the means of strengthening the bond of mutual effort between the adherents of the Buddhist religion and affording an immense contribution to the peace of the World and the welfare of mankind as expressed in the lofty ideals of the Holy Lord Buddha.

It is in order to perpetuate the memory of the present Conference that we have issued this English translation of the "New Translation of the Sacred Buddhist Scriptures." This work has been compiled and issued with a view to providing the younger English-speaking generation of the entire world with a suitable version of the sacred Buddhist Scriptures which are, in very truth, the spiritual nourishment of their daily life.

We have selected the original version of the popular edition of the "New Translation of the Sacred Buddhist Scriptures" compiled by the Buddhist Association of Nagoya City, as it is most appropriate to our purpose, being a synthesis of the most all-embracing Buddhist Scriptures, containing the quintessence of their precious teachings, and being in common use among all the Buddhist sects. Moreover, since a group of the most eminent Buddhist scholars in Japan collaborated in its compilation, it is, beyond all doubt, a model version of the Scriptures which can be used with all confidence by the adherents of the various sects of Buddhism in Japan.

As regards the present English translation, it is the product of the joint efforts of a number of Japanese Buddhist scholars of the highest order, while special mention should be made of the unsparing efforts of Mr. Dwight Goddard, an American, who devoted a stay of several months in this country to the bringing of the work to perfection and completion. It is our pleasant duty to pay a tribute of gratitude and respect from the bottom of our hearts to the pure and lofty devotion, as well as to the unstinted efforts, of this last-named gentleman.

In conclusion we must not forget to acknowledge our indebtedness to the many unrevealed, yet nonetheless precious, sacrifices and the economic assistance received from a large circle of co-religionists, to which this book owes its appearance.

The Federation of All
Young Buddhist Associations of Japan

July, the 2500th year of
Our Lord Buddha
(A.D. 1934)

SECTION ONE

BUDDHA

CHAPTER ONE

SAKYAMUNI BUDDHA

I

THE LIFE OF THE WORLD-HONORED ONE

1. THE Sakya clansmen dwelt along the river Rohini that flowed among the southern foothills of the Himalayas. Their King Suddhodana Gautama had transferred his capital to Kapila and there had built a great castle and had ruled wisely, winning the joyful acclaim of his people.

The Queen's name was Maya. She was the daughter of the King's uncle who was also a king of the neighboring division of the same Sakya clan. For twenty years they had no children, then, after dreaming a strange dream of an elephant entering her side, Queen Maya became pregnant. The King and the people looked forward with joyful expectancy to the birth of a royal child. According to their custom the Queen returned to her own home for the birth, and while on the way, in the beautiful spring sunshine, she rested in the flower garden of Lumbini Park. All about her were Asoka blossoms and in delight she reached out her right arm to pluck a branch and the Prince was born. All expressed their heart-felt delight and glory of the Queen and her princely child; even

Heaven and Earth manifested their joy.   This memorable day was the eighth day of April.   The joy of the King was extreme as he named the child: Siddhartha, which means, " Every wish fulfilled."

2.   In the palace of the King, however, delight was quickly followed by sorrow, for after a few days lovely Queen Maya suddenly passed away.   Fortunately her younger sister, Prajapati became the child's foster mother and brought it up with loving care.

A hermit, who lived in the mountains not far away, noticing a glory about the castle and interpreting it as a good omen, came down to the palace and was shown the child.   He predicted: " This Prince, if he remains in the palace after his youth, will become a great King to rule the Four Seas.   But if he forsakes the household life to embrace a religious life, he will become a Buddha and the world's Savior."   At first the King was pleased because of the prophecy, but later became troubled at the thought of the possibility of his only son leaving the palace to become a homeless recluse.

At the age of seven the Prince began his lessons in literature and the military arts, but his thoughts more naturally ran to other things.   One spring day he went out of the castle with his father and they were watching a farmer at his plowing; he noticed a bird flying down to the ground and carrying away a little worm which had been thrown out of the ground by the farmer's plough. He, who had lost his mother so soon after his birth, was deeply affected by the tragedy of these two little creatures. He sat down in the shade of a tree and thought about it, whispering to himself:

"Alas! Do all living creatures kill each other?"

This spiritual wound was deepened day after day as he grew up; like a little scar on a young tree, the sufferings of human life were more and more deeply carved into his mind.

The King was increasingly worried as he recalled the hermit's prophecy and tried in every possible way to cheer the Prince and to turn his thoughts in other directions. At the age of nineteen, the King arranged the marriage of the Prince to the Princess Yasodhara who was the daughter of Suprabuddha, Lord of Koliya castle and a brother of the late Queen Maya.

3. For ten years the Prince was immersed in a round of music, dancing and pleasure, in the different pavilions of Spring, Autumn and Winter, but ever his thoughts reverted to the problem of suffering as he pensively tried to understand the true meaning of human life.

"Luxuries of the palace, healthy bodies, rejoicing youth! what do they mean to me?" he meditated. "Some day we may be sick, we shall become aged, from death we can not eventually escape. Pride of youth, pride of health, pride of existence,—all thoughtful people must cast them aside."

"A man struggling for existence will naturally look for help. There are two ways of looking for help,—a right way and a wrong way.   To look the wrong way means that, while he recognises that sickness, old age and death are unavoidable, he looks for help among the same class of empty, transitory things.   To look the right way means that he recognises the true nature of sickness, old age and death, and looks for help in that which transcends all human suffering.   In this palace life of pleasure I seem to be looking for help in the wrong way."

4.   Thus the mental struggle went on in the mind of the Prince until his twenty-ninth year when his only child, Rahula, was born.   This seemed to bring things to a climax and he decided to leave his palace home and seek the solution of his mental unrest in the homeless life of a mendicant.   This plan he carried out one night, by leaving the castle with only his personal servant, Channa, and his favorite horse, the snow-white Kanthaka, and even these he left behind him when he had crossed the river at the bounds of his Father's kingdom.

But his mental troubles were not at an end and many doubts beset him.   " Perhaps it would be better for me to return to the castle and seek some other solution; then the whole world will be mine."   But he resisted these doubts by realising that nothing worldly could satisfy him.   So he shaved his head, carried a begging bowl in his hand, and turned his mendicant steps to the south.

The Prince first visited the hermit Bhagava and watched his ascetic practices; then he went successively to Arada Kalama and Udraka Ramaputra to learn their

methods of attainment, but after practising them for a time
he became convinced that they would not lead him to enlightenment.   Finally he went to the Magadha country
and practised asceticism in the forest of Uruvilva on the
banks of the Nairanjana river where it flows by the Gaya
Castle.

5.   The methods of his practice were unbelievably intense.
He spurred himself on with the thought that " no ascetic
in the past, none in the present, and none in the future,
ever have or ever will practise more earnestly than I do."

Still, the Prince could not get what he sought.   After
six years in the forest he gave up the practice of asceticism.
He bathed in the river and accepted a bowl of food from
the hand of Sujata, a maid who lived in the neighboring
village.   The five companions who had lived with the
Prince for the six years of his ascetic practices looked on
with amazement that he should receive food from the hand
of a maiden; they thought him degraded thereby and left
him.   The Prince, thus, was left alone.   He was still
feeble but at the risk of his life he attempted a final meditation, saying to himself, " Blood may become exhausted,
flesh may decay, bones may fall apart, but I will never
leave this place until I find the way to enlightenment."

It was an intense and incomparable struggle!   His
mind was desperate, was filled with confusing thoughts,
dark shadows overhung his spirit, he was beset with all
the lures of evil.   But carefully and patiently he examined
them one by one and rejected them all.   It, indeed, was

a hard struggle, that made his blood run thin, his flesh creep, and his bones crack.   But when the morning star appeared in the eastern sky, the struggle was over and the Prince's mind was as clear and bright as the day-break. He had found the path to enlightenment at last.   It was December the 8th, when he was thirty-five years of age that the Prince became Buddha.

6.   From this time on the Prince was known by different names: some spoke of him as Buddha, the Perfectly En-lightened One;   some spoke of him as Sakyamuni, the Sage of the Sakya clan;   others called him the World-honored One;   and still others spoke of him affectionately as the Blessed One.   He went first to Mrigadava in Vara-nasi where the five mendicants who had lived with him during the six years of his ascetic life were staying.   At first they shunned him, but after they had talked with him, they believed in him and became his first followers. Then he went to Rajagriha castle and won over King Bimbisara who had always been his friend.

From there he went about the country living on alms and persuading men to accept his way of life, and men responded to him as thirsty men seek water and hungry men seek food.   Two great teachers, Sariputra and Maudgalyayana, and two thousand disciples came to him. At first the Buddha's Father, King Suddhodana, suffering inwardly from his son's retirement, held aloof, but after-ward became his faithful disciple; and Maha-Prajapati, the Buddha's stepmother, and the Princess Yasodhara, his wife, and all the members of the Sakya clan, believed in him and followed him. And multitudes of others became his devotee and faithful followers.

7. For forty-five years the Buddha went about the country preaching and persuading men to follow his way of life, but at last, at Vaisali on the way from Rajagriha to Sravasti, he became ill and predicted that after three months he would enter Nirvana. Still he journeyed on until he reached Pava where he was made critically ill by food offered by Cunda, a blacksmith. Then by easy stages in spite of great pain and weakness, he reached the forest on the border of Kusinagara castle. Lying between two large sala trees, he continued his teachings to his favorite disciples until the last moment. Thus passed into the unknown the greatest of the world's teachers and the kindest of men.

8. Under the oversight of Ananda, the Buddha's favorite disciple, the body was cremated by his friends in Kusinagara castle. Seven of the neighboring rulers under the lead of King Ajatasatru demanded that the ashes be divided among them. The King of the Kusinagara castle at first refused and the dispute even threatened to end in a war, but by the advice of a wise man named Dona, the crisis passed and the ashes were divided and buried under eight great monuments. Even the embers of the fire and the earthern jar that had held the ashes were divided and given to two others to be likewise honored.

II

THE FINAL TEACHING OF THE BUDDHA

1. In his final words to his disciples under the sala trees, the Buddha uttered these words:

"Make my teaching your light! Rely upon it; do not depend upon any other teaching. Make of yourself a light. Rely upon yourself; do not depend upon anyone else."

"Consider your body; think of its impurity; how can you indulge its cravings as you see that both its pain and its delight are alike causes of suffering? Consider your soul; think of its transiency; how can you fall into delusion about it and cherish pride and selfishness, knowing that they must all end in inevitable suffering? Consider all substances; can you find among them any enduring "self"? Are they not all aggregates that sooner or later will break apart and be scattered? Do not be confused by the universality of suffering, but follow my teaching and you will be rid of pain. Do this and you will indeed be my disciples."

2. "My disciples. The teachings that I have given you are never to be forgotten nor abandoned. They are to be treasured, they are to be thought about, they are to be practised! If you follow these teachings you will always be happy."

"The point of the teachings is to control your own mind. Restrain your mind from greed, so shall you keep your body right, your mind pure, your words faithful.

Always thinking of the transiency of your life, you will be able to desist from greed and anger and will be able to keep clear from all evil.

"If you find your mind entangled in greed and tempted, you must suppress the greed and control the entangled mind; be the master of your own mind. A man's mind may make of him a Buddha, or it may make of him a beast. Being misled by error one becomes a demon; being enlightened one becomes a Buddha. Therefore keep your mind under control and do not let it deviate from the Noble Path."

3. "Under my teachings, brothers should respect each other and refrain from disputes; they should not repel each other like water and oil, but should mingle together like milk and water. Study together, learn together, practice the teachings together. Do not waste your mind and time in idleness and bickering. Enjoy the blossoms of enlightenment in their season and harvest the fruit of benevolence.

"The teachings which I have given you, I gained by following the path myself. You should follow the teachings and conform to their spirit on every occasion. If you neglect them it means that you have never really met me. It means that you are far from me even though are actually with me, but if you accept and practise my teachings then you are very near to me, even though you are far away."

4. "My disciples. The end is approaching, our parting is near, but do not lament. Life is ever changing; none

escape the dissolution of the body.   Now I am to manifest it by my own death, the body falling apart like a decayed cart. Do not vainly lament, but wonder at the rule of transiency and learn from it the emptiness of human life. Do not cherish the unworthy desire that the changeable might become unchanging. The demon of worldly desire is always seeking chances to deceive the mind. If a viper lives in your room, if you wish to have a peaceful sleep, you must chase it out. You must break the bonds of worldly passions and get rid of them as you would a viper."

5. " My disciples. The last moment has come, but do not forget that death is but the vanishing of a body. The body was born from parents and was nourished by food, so sickness and death is unavoidable. But the true Buddha is not a human body:—it is Enlightenment. A human body must vanish, but the wisdom of Enlightenment will exist forever in the truths of the Dharma, and in the practice of the Dharma. He who sees my body only, is not the one who truly sees me. He who accepts my teachings, is the one who truly sees me. After my death, the Dharma shall be your teacher. Follow the Dharma and you will be true to me.

" During the last forty-five years of my life I have kept back nothing from my teaching. There is no secret teaching, no hidden meaning, everything has been taught openly and clearly.

" My dear disciples; this is the end.   In a moment I shall be passing into Nirvana."

CHAPTER TWO

THE ETERNAL AND GLORIFIED BUDDHA

I

ITS COMPASSION AND VOWS

(Buddha is thought of in two aspects: His earthly body of manifestation and the Bliss-body of Reward with all its boundless potentiality for Love and Wisdom.)

1. THE spirit of Buddha is a great compassion and love to save all people by any and all means. It is the spirit of a mother toward her child nourishing and protecting it; it is the spirit that prompts it to be ill with the sickness of people, to suffer with their suffering. "Your suffering is my suffering and your happiness is my happiness," said Buddha, and he does not forget that spirit for a single moment, for it is the self-nature of Buddhahood to be compassionate. A mother realises her motherhood by loving her child; then the child reacting to its mother's love feels safe and at ease. The Buddha's spirit of compassion is stimulated according to the need of a man ; man's faith is the reaction to this spirit, and it leads him to enlightenment.

Yet the people do not understand this spirit of Buddha and go on suffering from the illusions and desires that spring from their ignorance; they suffer from the karma accumulated by worldly passions, and wander about among the mountains of delusion with a heavy burden of pain.

2.   Do not think that the compassion of the earthly Buddha is only for the present life; that was only a manifestation of the timeless compassion of the eternal Buddha that has been operative since mankind first went astray from ignorance.   The eternal Buddha ever appears before people in most friendly forms and brings to them the wisest methods of relief.

Sakyamuni Buddha was born a Prince among his Sakya kinsmen, he left the comforts of his home to practise asceticism, then by Dhyana he realised enlightenment, he preached it among his kinsmen and finally manifested an earthly death.   Yet this was nothing but one of Buddha's manifestations of compassion.   The task of Buddahood is as everlasting as human life is everlasting; and as the depth of ignorance is bottomless, so Buddha's compassion is boundless.

When Buddha decided to break from the worldly life, he made four great vows:—To save all people; to renounce all worldly desires; to learn all the teachings; and to attain perfect enlightenment.   These vows were not original with him,—they were but a manifestation of the love and compassion that is fundamental in the self-nature of Buddhahood.

3.   Buddha first trained himself to be kind to all animate

life and to avoid the sin of killing any living creature, and then he wished for all people that they might have the blessedness of a long life. The Buddha trained himself to avoid the sin of stealing, and then he wished for all people that they might have everything they wanted. Buddha trained himself to avoid impure thoughts, and then with its virtuous deed he wished for all people that they might know the blessedness of a pure spirit and not suffer from unsatisfied desires. Buddha, aiming at his ideal, trained himself to keep free from all deception, and then by its virtuous deed he wished for all people that they might know the tranquillity of mind that follows speaking the truth. He trained himself to avoid all duplicity, and then wished for all people that they might know the joy of fellowship among those who follow his teaching. He trained himself to avoid abusing others, and then he wished for everybody that they might have the peaceful mind that follows living at peace with others. He kept himself free from idle talk, and then wished for everybody that they might know the blessedness of understanding sympathy.

The Buddha, aiming at his ideal, trained himself to keep free from greed, and then by its virtuous deed he wished for all people that they might know the peacefulness that goes with freedom from all greed. He trained himself to avoid anger, and then he wished for all people that they might love one another. He trained himself to understand the true significance of things and not to be stupid, and then he wished for all people that they might understand Karma and not disregard it.

Thus Buddha's compassion embraces all people and his never lessening desire is for their happiness. He loves people as parents love their children and he wishes for them the highest blessedness, namely, that they might be able to pass beyond this ocean of life and death.

II

BUDDHA'S RELIEF AND HIS METHOD OF RELIEF

1. It is very difficult for the words of the Buddha spoken on the thither bank of Enlightenment to reach the people struggling in the sea of delusion, so Buddha crosses the sea himself and applies his method of relief.

"Now I will tell you a fable," Buddha says: "Once there lived a wealthy man whose house was on fire. The rich man was absent and when he came back home, found that the children absorbed in play, had not noticed the fire but remained inside.

"The father called to them: 'Run children; come out of the house; hurry!'

"But the children did not heed him, so the anxious father shouted again: 'Children; I have some wonderful toys here, come out of the house and get them!' Heeding his cry this time, the children escaped from the burning house."

This world is a burning house, but the people unaware that the house is on fire are in danger of being burned to death.   So Buddha in compassion devises ways of saving them.

2. Buddha said:—" I will tell you another parable. Once upon a time the only son of a wealthy man left his home and fell into extreme poverty. The father moving away from the old home, they lost track of each other. The father did everything he could to find the son but in vain. In the course of time the son, now reduced to wretchedness, wandered near where the father was living. The father recognised his son and sent his servants to bring the wanderer home, but the son was suspicious and feared a trick and would not go with them. Then the father sent his servants again and told them to offer his son money to become a servant in the rich man's house. The son accepted this offer and returned with the servants to the father's house and became a servant. The father gradually advanced him until he had charge of all the father's property and treasures, but still the son did not recognise his own father.

  " The father was pleased with his son's faithfulness, and as the end of his life drew near, he called together his relatives and friends and said to them:—Friends, this is my only son, the son I have been seeking for many years. From now on, all my property and treasures belong to him.

  The son was surprised at his father's confession and said:—" Not only have I found my father but all this property and treasures are mine."

Buddha's compassion embraces all people with the love of a father for an only son.   In that love he conceives the wisest methods to lead, teach and enrich them with all his treasures.

3. Just as rain falls alike on all vegetation, so Buddha's compassion extends equally to all people; but just as different plants receive particular benefits from the same rain, so people of different nature and circumstances are blessed by different methods.

4. Parents love all their children, but their love is expressed with particular tenderness toward a sick child. Buddha's compassion is equal toward all people, but it is expressed with especial care toward those who have a heavier load of evil and suffering to bear because of their ignorance.

The sun rises in the eastern sky and clears away the darkness of the world without any prejudice toward any substance or any favoritism. So Buddha's compassion encompasses all people to encourage them in the right and to guide them against evil; thus he clears away the darkness of ignorance and leads the people to enlightenment.   Buddha is a father in mercy and a mother in compassion.   In their ignorance and bondage to worldly desire they often act like crazy people,—Buddha out of compassion for them acts like a crazy man, too.   They are helpless without Buddha's compassion; they should receive his methods of relief with the teachableness of children.

III

THE ETERNAL BUDDHA

1. Common people believe that Buddha was born a prince and learned the path of enlightenment as a mendicant, but in fact, there had been a long, long preparation, for Buddha has always existed in a beginningless world. As Eternal Buddha he has known all people and applied all methods of relief. Though the teaching varies from age to age, its aim is always the same:—to lead all people to rid themselves of delusions. There is no falsity in the Eternal Dharma, for Buddha knows the world and all things as they truly are, and Buddha teaches all people.

Indeed it is very difficult to understand the world as it truly is, for it is not real though it seems so and it is not false though it seems so. Ignorant people can not know the truth concerning the world. Buddha alone truly and fully understands it and he never says that it is real or false, or good or evil, as it exists in itself. He simply points out the world as it is. But what Buddha does teach is this:—that all people should cultivate roots of virtue according to the nature, the deed and the belief of people. This Dharma surpasses all affirmation and all negation as to the world in itself.

2. Buddha teaches not only in words, he demonstrates by his life. He demonstrates that life is endless, and then

to teach people who are greedy for eternal life, he uses the method of birth and death, to awaken their attention.

" While a physician was away from his home his children tasted of a poison. When the physician returned, he noticed their sickness and prepared an antidote. Some of the children who were not seriously poisoned accepted the medicine and were cured, but others were so seriously affected that they refused to take the medicine, preferring the poison to the cure. The physician, prompted by his father-love for his children, decided on an extreme method to get them to take the cure. He said to the children: I must go away on a distant journey. I am old and may pass away any day. If I am with you I can care for you, but if I should pass away, you will become worse and worse, if you hear of my death. I implore you to take the antidote and be cured of this subtle poisoning. Then he went away on the long journey.

" After a time, he sent a messenger to his children to inform them of his death. The children receiving the message were deeply affected by the thought of their father's death and that they would no longer have the benefit of his thoughtful care. They recalled his parting request of them and because of their sorrow and feeling of helplessness, they took the medicine and recovered."

People may condemn the deception of this father-physician, but Buddha is like that father: he, too, employs the fiction of life and death to persuade people, who are immersed in the bondage of desire, to take this the only means to break the bondage. And the Eternal Buddha is very wise and kind-hearted, and has lived a very long time.

CHAPTER THREE

THE FORM OF BUDDHA AND HIS VIRTUES

I

BUDDHA'S THREE BODIES

1. Do not seek to know Buddha by his form and attributes; for neither the form nor attributes are the real Buddha. The true Buddha is Enlightenment itself. Therefore aspiration to realise Enlightenment is the true way to know Buddha.

If anyone after seeing an excellent image of Buddha thinks that he knows Buddha, it is a mistake of dull eyes, for the true Buddha can not be embodied in form or seen by human eyes. Neither can one know Buddha by a faultless description of his attributes. It has never been found possible to describe his attributes in human words. Though we speak of his form, the Eternal Buddha has no form, but he can manifest himself in any form. Though we describe his attributes, yet the Eternal Buddha has no attributes, but he can manifest himself in any and all attributes. So if any one sees distinctly the form of Buddha, or visions his attributes clearly, and yet does not become attached to the form or to the attributes, he has the capacity to see and know Buddha.

2. Buddha's body is Enlightenment itself. Being form-less and substanceless it always has been and always will be. It is not a physical body that has had a beginning and must be nourished by food. It is an ethereal body whose substance is Wisdom. Buddha has no disease; he is eternally changeless.

Therefore Buddha will never disappear as long as the path to Enlightenment exists. Enlightenment appears as a light of Wisdom on the path that awakens people into a newness of life and causes them to be reborn into the likeness of Buddhahood. Those who are thus quickened become the children of Buddha; they keep his Dharma, honor his teachings and pass them on to posterity. Nothing can be more miraculous nor more natural than the power of Buddha.

3. Buddhahood has three aspects. There is an aspect of Essence which is all-inclusive, universal and inconceivable; there is an aspect of Potentiality which is boundless but unmanifest; and there is an aspect of Manifestation which is both activity and changeless Peace. As Essence it is the substance of the Dharma; that is, it is the substance of Truth as it is in itself. As Potentiality it is the Dharma considered as the Truth Principle, potent but unmanifest; it is the glorified Compensation Body of Buddhahood. As Manifestation it is Buddhahood manifesting itself in the temporal bodies of Sakyamuni Buddha and other earthly Buddha.

As the aspect of Essence, Buddha has no figure

nor color, and since he has no form nor color, Buddha
comes from nowhere and there is nowhere for him to
go. Like the blue sky he overarches everything, and
since he is all things he lacks nothing. He exists not
because people think that he does or as they think, neither
does he disappear because people forget him. He is under
no particular compulsion to appear when people are happy
and comfortable, neither is it necessary for him to disappear when people are inattentive and idle. Buddha
transcends every conceivable trend of human thought;
Buddha's body fills every corner of the universe; it reaches
everywhere, it exists forever, regardless of whether people
believe in him or doubt his existence.

4. The aspect of Potentiality signifies that in the nature
of Buddha there is the merging of both Compassion
and Wisdom into one imageless spirit, that is capable
of both manifesting this imageless spirit under the symbols
of bitrh and death, ignorance and enlightenment, and
then under the symbols of making vows and undergoing
training he leads all people and saves them. Thus compassion is the Essence of the Dharma and in its spirit
Buddha uses all manner of skilful devices to emancipate
as many people as are ready for emancipation. Like a
fire that once kindled never dies away until the fuel is
consumed, so the Compassion of Buddha never fails
until all worldly passion is consumed away. Just as
a wind blows away the dust, so the compassion of Buddha
blows away the dust of human suffering.

The aspect of Manifestation signifies that in order to complete the relief of Buddha of potentiality, the Buddha appeared in flesh in the world, and showed the people the aspect of the birth, renunciation and obtaining of the Enlightenment, also according to their natures and capacities. Buddha teaches the Dharma and then applies all manner of skilful means to lead them. There is birth and ignorance and discrimination and suffering and death, but with them go awakening faith, knowledge and enlightenment.

5. The form of Buddha is the image of the Dharma, but as the nature of people varies, Buddha's form appears differently. Although the form of Buddha varies according to the different desires, tasks and faculties of people, Buddha is concerned only with the truth of the Dharma. Though Buddha has different aspects, his spirit or purpose is one, and that the purpose is to save all people.

Though in all circumstances Buddha is manifest in his purity, yet the manifestation is not Buddha because Buddha is not form. Buddhadood fills everything, making enlightenment his body and as enlightenment he appears before all those who have capacity to realise Truth.

II
THE APPEARANCE OF BUDDHA

1. It is seldom that a Buddha appears in the world.

When a Buddha does appear, he establishes Enlightenment, introduces the Dharma, cuts the net of suspicion, removes the lure of desire at its root, plugs the fountain of evil; and unhindered by anything, walks where he will over all the world. There is no greater merit than to recognise a Buddha and pay reverence to him and learn from him. Buddha appears in the world because he can not desert suffering people; his only purpose is to spread the Dharma and to bless all people with its Truth.

It is very difficult to introduce the Dharma into a world filled with injustice and false standards, a world that is vainly struggling with insatiable desires and discomforts. Buddha is facing these difficulties because of his great love and compassion.

2.   Buddha is a friend of every one in this world. If Buddha finds a man suffering under a heavy burden of worldly passions, he has sympathy for the man and shares the burden with him. If he meets a man suffering from delusions, he will clear away the man's illusions by the pure light of his wisdom. Like a calf which enjoys living with its mother, those who have heard the Buddha's teachings are afterward unwilling to leave him because his teachings bring them happiness.

3.   When the moon disappears, people say that the moon has gone; and when the moon reappears, they say that the moon has come. But, in fact, the moon never goes nor comes, but shines changelessly in the sky. Buddha

is exactly like the moon:—he neither appears nor disappears; he only seems to do so, out of love for the people that he may teach them.

At one phase of the moon's appearance, people speak of it as the full-moon; and at another phase, they call it a crescent, but the moon itself is always perfectly round, never waxing nor waning. Buddha is precisely like the moon. In the eyes of people Buddha may seem to change in appearance, but in truth, Buddha changes not. The moon appears everywhere, over a crowded city, a sleepy village, a mountain, a river; it is seen in the depths of a pond, in a jug of water, in a drop of dew on a leaf. If a man walks hundreds of miles the moon goes with him. The moon does not change, but to people it seems to change. Buddha is like the moon in following the people of this world in all their changing circumstances, but in his Essence he changes not. It is because of the compassion and wisdom of Buddha that he employs the device of causes and conditions to lead them to faith in his unchangeableness.

4.   The fact that Buddha appears and disappears can be explained by causality:—Namely, when the conditions are propitious, Buddha appears; when conditions are unpropitious, Buddha seems to disappear from the world. But whether Buddha appears or disappears, Buddhahood always remains the same. Knowing this principle the wise will keep to the path of Enlightenment and Perfect Wisdom, undisturbed by the apparent changes in the

image of Buddha and in the conditions of the world and in the fluctuations of human thought.

It has been explained that Buddha is not body but is Enlightenment. Body may be thought of as a receptacle; then, if this receptacle is filled with Enlightenment, it may be called Buddha. But, if anyone falls into the belief that Buddha is a body external to himself and laments his disappearance, he will be unable to realise the real Buddha.

In reality, all things are empty of all aspects of appearing and disappearing, of comings and goings, of differentiations of this and that, of good and evil. All things are perfect emptiness and perfect homogeneity. It is because of the combination of a principle cause, of other contributing causes, and of all other conditions, that delusion as to the form of Buddha and as to his attributes, arises and disappears. But the true form of Buddha never appears nor disappears.

III

BUDDHA'S VIRTUE

1. Buddha receives the respect of the world because of five virtues:—Superior conduct; superior point of view; perfect wisdom; superior preaching ability; and the power to lead people to the practice of his teaching.

Buddha has also eight other virtues:—He bestows blessings and happiness upon people; the practice of his teaching brings immediate benefit in this world; he rightly adjudicates between good and bad, right and wrong; by teaching the right way he leads people to enlightenment; he leads all people by an equal way; in Buddha there is no boasting; He willingly completes his spiritual practices and by so doing fulfills the vows of his compassionate heart.

By the practice of meditation, Buddha preserves a calm and peaceful spirit radiant with mercy, compassion and happiness. He deals equitably with all people, clearing away their defilement of mind and bestowing happiness in perfect singleness of spirit.

2. Buddha is both father and mother to the people of the world. For many months after a child is born the father and mother have to speak with it in childish words, then they gradually teach him better words. Like earthly parents, Buddha first cares for people and then leaves them to care for themselves; he first brings to pass according to their desires and then he brings them to a peaceful and safe shelter.

What Buddha preaches in his language, people receive and assimilate in their own language as if it was specially intended for them. Buddha's horizon surpasses human thought; it can not be made clear by words or examples, it can only be hinted at in parables.

A little brook is muddled by the tramping of horses and cows and is disturbed by the movement of fish and turtles, but a great river flows on pure and undisturbed by such trifles. Buddha is like a great river. The fish and turtles of other teachings swim about in its depths and push against its current but in vain; Buddha's Dharma flows on pure and undisturbed.

3. Buddha's Wisdom being perfect keeps away from the extremes of prejudice and preserves moderation beyond all words to describe. Being all-wise he knows the thoughts and feelings of people and appreciates all their circumstances.

As the stars of the heavens are reflected in a calm sea, so people's thoughts, feelings and circumstances are reflected in the depths of Buddha's Wisdom. This is why Buddha is called, The Perfectly Enlightened One. Buddha's Wisdom refreshes the arid minds of people, enlightens them and teaches them the singificance of this world, its causes and its effects, its appearings and disappearings. Indeed, apart from Buddha's Wisdom, what aspects of the world can be understood at all?

4. Buddha does not always appear as a Buddha. Sometimes he appears as an incarnation of evil, sometimes as a woman, a god, a king, a statesman; sometimes he appears in a brothel or in a gambling house, and in an epidemic he appears as a physician bringing healing; but always he is preaching and manifesting the Dharma, for the emancipation of the world. In a war he preaches forbearance and mercy for the sufferings of people; for those who are content with things as they are, he preaches transiency and uncertainty; for those who are proud and egoistic,

he preaches humility and self-sacrifice; for those who are entangled in the web of worldly pleasures, he reveals the misery of the world.

The task of Buddha is to manifest in all affairs and on all occasions the pure essence of Dharmarkaya; so Buddha's mercy and compassion flow out from the same Dharmakaya in endless lives and boundless light bringing salvation. The world is like a burning house that is forever being destroyed and forever being rebuilt. People being confused by the darkness of ignorance lose their minds in anger, displeasure, jealousy, prejudice, and worldly passion. They are like babies needing a mother; everyone is dependent upon Buddha's mercy.

5. Buddha is a father to all the world; all human beings are children of Buddha; Buddha is the most saintly of saints. The world is afire with decrepitude and death; there is suffering everywhere, but people being engrossed in the vain search for worldly pleasure are not wise enough to fully realise it. Buddha saw that his palace of pleasure was really a burning house, so he fled from it and found refuge and peace in the quiet forest. There, in its solitude and silence, a great heart of compassion came to him and he learned to say: " This world of change and suffering is my world; these ignorant, heedless people are my children; I am the only one who can save them from their delusion and misery."

As Buddha is the great king of Dharma, he can preach to all people as he wishes; so Buddha appears in the world to bless the people, and to save them from suffering he preaches the Dharma, but the ears of people are dulled by greed and they are heedless. But those who listen to his teachings are free from the delusions and the miseries of life. "People can not be saved by relying on their own wisdom," he said, "they must enter into my Dharma through faith." Therefore, one should listen to Buddha's Dharma and put it into practice.

SECTION TWO

DHARMA

CHAPTER ONE

CAUSATION

I

THE FOUR NOBLE TRUTHS

1. THE world is full of suffering. Birth is suffering, decrepitude is suffering, so are sickness and death suffering. To face a man of hatred is suffering, to be separated from a beloved one is suffering, or to be vainly struggling to satisfy one's needs. In fact, life that is not free from desire and passion is always involved with suffering. This is called the Truth of Suffering.

The cause of human suffering is undoubtedly found in the thirsts of the physical organism and in the illusions of worldly passion. If these thirsts and illusions are traced to their source, they are found to be rooted in the intense desires of physical instincts. Thus desire, having a strong will-to-live at its basis, goes after what is sensed as being desirable. Sometimes desire even turns toward death. This is called the Truth of the Cause of Suffering.

If desire which lies at the root of all human passion can be removed, then passion will die out and all human suffering will be ended. This is called the Truth of the Ending of Suffering.

In order to enter into a condition where there is no desire and no suffering, one must follow a certain Path.

The stages of this Noble Path are:—Right Ideas, Right Resolution, Right Speech, Right Behavior, Right Vocation, Right Effort, Right Mindfulness, Right Concentration. This is called the Truth of the Noble Path to the Ending of Desire.

People should keep these Truths clearly in mind, for the world is filled with suffering and if anyone wishes to escape from suffering they must cut the ties of worldly passion which is the sole cause of suffering. The way of life which is free from all worldly passion and suffering can only be known by enlightenment, and elightenment can only be gained by the discipline of the Noble Path.

2. All those who are seeking enlightenment, must understand these Four Noble Truths. Without this understanding, they will wander about for a long time in the bewildering maze of life's illusions. Those who understand the Four Noble Truths are called: " The people who have acquired the eyes of enlightenment." Therefore, people who wish to follow the Buddha's taechings should concentrate their minds on these Four Noble Truths and seek to make their meaning clear. In all ages, a saint, if he is a true saint, is one who understands them and teaches them to others.

When the Four Noble Truths are clearly understood, then the Noble Path will lead them away from greed; and if they are free from greed they will not quarrel with the world, they will not act indecently, nor kill, nor steal, nor cheat, nor abuse, nor flatter, nor envy, nor lose their temper, nor forget the transciency of life; nor will they err in justice.

3. Following the Noble Path is like entering a dark room with a light in the hand; the darkness will all be cleared away, and the room will be filled with light. People who understand the meaning of the Noble Truths and have learned to follow the Noble Path are in possession of a light of wisdom that will clear away the darkness of ignorance. Buddha leads the people, by only following the Four Noble Truths. Those who understand it properly will gain enlightenment; they will be able to guide and support others in the bewildering world, and they will be worthy of trust. When the Four Noble Truths are clearly understood, the sources of all worldly passion are dried up. Advancing from these Four Noble Truths, the disciples of Buddha will attain all other precious truths, will gain the wisdom and piety to understand all meanings, and will become able to preach the Dharma to all the people of all the world.

II

CAUSATION

1. There are causes for all human suffering, and there is a way by which they may be ended, because everything in the world is the result of a vast concurrence of causes and conditions, and everything disappears as these causes and conditions change and pass away. Rain falls, wind

blows, plants bloom, leaves mature and are blown away; these phenomena are all interrelated with causes and conditions, are brought about by them, and disappear as the cuases and conditions change.

A child is born by the conditions of parentage; its body is nourished by food, its spirit is nurtured by teaching and experience. Therefore, both flesh and spirit are related to conditions and are changed as conditions change. A net is made up by a series of ties, so everything in this world is connected by a series of ties. If any one thinks that a mesh of a net is an independent, isolated thing, he is mistaken. It is called a net because it is made up of a series of connected meshes, and each mesh has its place and responsibilities in relation to other meshes.

2. Blossoms bloom because of a series of conditions that lead up to blooming; leaves are blown away because a series of conditions lead up to it. Blossoms do not bloom unconditioned, nor does a leaf fall of itself. So everything has its appearing and passing away; nothing remains unchanged.

It is the everlasting and unchanging rule of this world that everything is created by a series of causes and conditions and everything disappears by the same rule; everything changes, nothing remains unchanged.

III

THE CHAIN OF CAUSATION

1. What, then, is the source of human grief, lamentation, pain and agony? Is it not to be found in the fact that people are generally ignorant and wilful? They cling obstinately to a life of wealth, honor, comfort, pleasure, excitement and egoism, ignorant of the fact that it is from the desire for these very things that human suffering starts. From its beginning, the world has been filled with a succession of calamities, besides there are the unavoidable facts of illness, decrepitude and death. But if one considers all the facts carefully, he must be convinced that at the base of all suffering lies the principle of ignorance and desire. If ignorance and desire can be removed, human suffering will come to an end.

The principle of ignorance is manifested in the obscurities and false imaginations that fill the human mind. These obscurities and false imaginations rise from the fact that people ignore the emptiness and transitoriness of life and are ignorant of the right reason for the succession of things. From these obscurities and false imaginations there spring impure desires for things that are in fact unobtainable, but for which they restlessly and blindly search. Because of these false imaginations and impure desires, people imagine discriminations where, among things themselves, there are no discriminations. Among the acts of human behavior, inherently, there are no discriminations of right and wrong, but people because of ignorance imagine they see distinctions and discriminate them as right and wrong, all because of the obscurities of false imaginations and impure desires.

Because of their ignorance, people are always thinking wrong thoughts and always losing the right view point, and then, by changing to their supposed ego-personality, they take wrong action and as a result grasp and become attached to a whole body of delusion.   But, in fact, there is no such thing as an ego-personality, except as it is imagined by the mind in an effort to synthesize its sensual and instinctive desires.   Making their karma the field of an ego-personality, using the activities of the mind as seed, beclouding the mind by ignorance, fertilizing it with the rain of impure desires, irrigating by the wilfulness of an ego-personality, they add the conception of evil, and bear about this incarnation of delusions.

2.   Ultimately this body of delusion is their own mind and, therefore, it is their own mind which causes the delusion of grief, lamentation, pain and agony.   This whole world of delusion is nothing but the shadow caused by this mind, and for the same reason, the world of enlightenment also appears from this same mind.

3.   In this world there are three wrong view points, if one clings to these view points, then everything in the world must be denied.   First, some people maintain the idea that all human experience is based on destiny; second, some hold that everything is created by God and

controlled by his will; third, some say that everything happens by chance.

If all has been decided by destiny, both good deeds and evil deeds are destiny, weal and woe are destiny, and nothing exists outside destiny, then all human plans and effort for improvement and progress would be in vain and humanity would be without hope. The same is true of the other conceptions, for, if everything in the last resort is in the hands of God or of blind chance, what hope has humanity except in submission? It is no wonder that people holding these conceptions lose hope and relax their effort to act wisely and avoid evil. No, these three conceptions and viewpoints are all wrong:—everything is a succession of appearances whose source is the concurrence of causes and conditions, and these causes and conditions can, in a measure, be modified and controlled.

CHAPTER TWO

THE THEORY OF MIND-ONLY
AND ACTUALITY

I

UNCERTAINTY AND EGOLESSNESS

1. THOUGH both body and mind appear because of co-operating cause, it does not follow that there is an ego-personality. As the body of flesh is an aggregate of elements, it is, therefore, impermanent. If the body was an ego-personality, it could do this and that as it determined. A king has the power to praise or punish as he wishes, but a person becomes ill against his intent and desire, he comes to old age unwillingly, and his fortune and his wishes often have little to do with each other.

Neither is the mind the ego-personality. The human mind is also an aggregate of causalities and relations. It is in constant change. If the mind was an ego-personality it could do this and that as it determined, but the mind often flies from what it knows is right and chases after evil unwillingly. Nothing seems to happen exactly as the ego desires.

2. If the body is asked whether there is constancy or uncertainty, it would be obliged to answer, uncertainty. If the uncertainty is asked whether it is to be happiness or

suffering, it will generally have to answer suffering.   But
if a man believes that such uncertainty, so changeable and
replete with suffering, is the possession of an ego-personality, he makes a serious mistake.

The human mind is also uncertainty and suffering, it
has nothing to be called an ego-personality.   Therefore,
both body and mind which make up an individual life,
and the external world which seems to surround him, are
far removed from both the conceptions of an ego and from
" my possession."   It is simply the mind clouded over
by impure desires, and thus impervious to wisdom, that
obstinately persists in thinking of " myself " and " my
possession."

Since both body and its surroundings are created by
cooperating causes, they are continually changing and
never can come to an end.   The human mind in its never-
ending change is like the moving water of a river, is like
the burning flame of a candle, is like an ape, forever jumping about, never ceasing for a moment.   A wise man,
seeing this, should break away from any attachment to
the body or mind, if he is ever to attain enlightenment.

3.   There are five facts which no one is able to accomplish:—first, to cease getting aged when he is actually getting aged; second, to cease being sick when he is actually
sick; third, to cease dying when he is actually dying;
fourth, to deny dissolution when there is actual dissolution; fifth, to deny extinction when it is already extinction.
All people in the world sooner or later run into these facts

and most people suffer in consequence of them, but those
who have acquired Buddha's teaching do not suffer because they understand that they are unavoidable facts.

Then there are four truths that can not be changed
and are unavoidable also:—first, all sentient life rises from
ignorance; second, the consequence of all impure desire
is endless change, uncertainty and suffering; third, the
existing facts are also change, uncertainty and suffering;
fourth, there is nothing that can be called an " ego ", and
there is no " idea of mine " in all the world. These facts,
that everything is empty and passing and egoless, have no
connection with the fact of Buddha's appearing or not appearing. These facts and truths are incontrovertible;
the Buddha knows this and therefore preaches the Dharma
to all people.

II

THE FACT OF MIND-ONLY

1. Both delusion and enlightenment originate within the
mind, and every fact arises from the activities of mind, just
as different things appear from the sleeve of a magician.
The activities of the mind have no limit and form the
surroundings of the life. An impure mind surrounds itself with impure things and a pure mind surrounds itself
with pure surroundings, hence surroundings have no more
limits than have the activities of the mind. When an artist
draws a picture the details are filled in from his own mind
and a single picture is capable of an infinite variety of de-

tails, so the human mind fills in the surroundings of its life, there is nothing in the world that is not mind-created, and just as the human mind creates, so Buddha creates and all other beings act as Buddha acts, so in the great task of creation the human mind, Buddha and all other beings are alike active.

2. But the mind that creates its surroundings is never free from their shadow; it remembers and fears and laments, not only the past but the present and future because they have arisen out of ignorance and greed. It is out of ignorance and greed that the world of delusion starts and all the vast complex of co-ordinating causes and conditions exist within the mind and nowhere else. Both life and death arise from mind and exist within the mind and hence when the mind that concerns itself with life and death passes, the world of life and death passes with it.

An unenlightened and bewildered life rises out of a mind that is bewildered by its own creation of a world of delusion. As they learn that there is no world of delusion outside of the mind, the bewildered mind becomes clear and as they cease to create impure surroundings they attain enlightenment. Thus the world of life and death is created by mind, is in bondage to mind, is ruled by mind; and the mind is master of every situation. As the wheels follow the ox that draws the cart, so suffering follows the mind that surrounds itself with impure thoughts and worldly passions.

3.   But if a man speaks and acts by a good mind, happiness follows him as a man's shadow.   Those who act in evil, selfish ways suffer not only from the natural consequences of the acts, but are followed by the thought, " I have done wrong," and the memory of the act is stored in karma to work out its inevitable retribution in following lives.   But those who act from good motives are made happy by the thought, " I have done a good act " and are made happier by the thought that the good act will bring continuing happiness in endless lives to follow.

If a mind is impure it will cause the feet to stumble on a rough and difficult road with many a fall and much pain; but if the mind is pure the path will be smooth and the journey peaceful.   If one is to enjoy a smooth and peaceful path he must cultivate his Buddha-mind, breaking the net of selfish impure thoughts and evil desires.

III

IDEAS-ONLY

1.   Everything originates within the mind.   Just as a magician cleverly makes whatever he wishes to appear, so this world of delusion originates within the mind.   People look upon it and observe its appearing and disappearing and they believe it to be real and call it life and death. That is, everything is mind-made and has no significance apart from mind.   As people come to understand this fact, they are able to remove all delusions and there is an end of all mental disturbance forever.

The human mind may be thought of as functioning on three different levels of cognition. On its lowest level it is a discriminating mind; on this level it has the ability to see, hear, taste, smell, touch, to combine these sense concepts, to discriminate them, and to consider their relations. On a higher level it is an intellectual mind where it has the ability to make the inward adjustments that are necessary to harmonise the reactions of the discriminating mind and to relate them to each other and to a whole ego conception. On its highest level it is Universal Mind. As Universal Mind it is pure, tranquil, unconditioned, in its true essential nature, but because of its relation to the lower minds it becomes the storage for their reactions and is defiled by them.

2. The human mind discriminates itself from the things that appear to be outside itself without realising that it has first created these very things within its own mind. This has been going on since beginningless time and the delusion has become firmly fixed within the mind, and even adheres to the things themselves. Because of this discrimination between the self and the not-self the mind has come to consider itself as an ego-personality and has become attached to it as being something different and more enduring than the things of the world. Thus, the people of the world grow up in ignorance of the fact that discrimination and thinking of ego-personality are nothing but activities of universal mind.

Universal Mind, while remaining pure and tranquil

and unconditioned in its self-nature, is the source of all mental processes and is, thus, the foundation for the other two minds and retains within itself all their experiences. The Mind, therefore, like a waterfall, never ceases its activity.   Just as a peaceful ocean suddenly becomes a tumult of waves because of some passing tempest, so the ocean of Mind becomes stirred by tempests of delusion and winds of karma.   And just as the ocean again becomes peaceful when the tempest passes, so the Ocean of Mind resumes its natural calm when the winds of karma and delusion are stilled.

3.   The body and its surroundings are all alike manifestations of the one mind, but as observed by human eyes they appear to be different and they are classified as " observer " and as " things observed."   But as nothing in the world exists apart from mind, there can be no essential difference between subject and object.   The ego-self and the idea of possession have no true existence.   There is only the age-old habit of erroneous thinking that leads people to perceive and to discriminate various aspects of the world where, in reality, there are none.   All objects, all words, all facts in the world, this body, this treasure, this dwelling, are all appearances that have arisen because of the activities of delusions that are inherent within their own mental processes.

If people can change their view-points, can break up these age-old habits of thinking, can rid their minds of the desires and infatuations of egoism, then the wisdom of

true enlightenment is possible. If they can bring themselves to understand that everything is only manifestations
of their own minds, if they can only keep their minds free
from being confused by appearances and deceived by
images, then it is possible to gain true enlightenment.
The enlightenment preached by Buddha is the true enlightenment. It comes and can only come when the mind
is pure of all defilement and clear from all perverting ideas
concerning the self and its surroundings.

4.   Thus the world of delusion and the world of enlightenment are from the same mind. The effort to keep the
mind clear from discriminating ideas so that it can rightly
understand the true nature of enlightenment, is the path
to enlightenment, every circumstance is right and every
dwelling place is in Buddha's Land of Purity.

In reality all Buddha-lands are designed to be a bles-
sing to people, because people's minds and Buddha-lands
are all of the same nature. It is like a house built upon a
good foundation. Wherever people live, that is Buddha's Pure Land. But the Land of Buddha must be built
upon by pure minds. The pure mind must at the same
time be a deep mind, if it is to follow successfully the path
to enlightenment. It must be the soul of compassion and
charity, it must observe the precepts, it must be patient
and humble, it must be earnest and persevering, it must
be tranquil and peaceful, it must be the soul of wisdom,
as well as the soul of compassion, the soul that is earnest
to use wise and kindly means and methods to bring all

people to enlightenment.

5.   If people wish to make a Buddha-land of this world, they must first cleanse their own minds.   If minds are pure, surroundings will be pure.   If surroundings are clean and minds are pure, this world will be a house for Buddha.   Then, someone will ask, why is this world so crowded with impurities?

A blind man can not see the sun nor the moon, but that is no reason why he should deny the existence of the sun and the moon.   When people have impure minds they are blind to the true nature of things; they can not see the purity that is all about them in this world.   In those who have a pure and transparent mind there will be an eye of wisdom with which they will be able to recognise, even in this world, Buddha's Land of Purity.

IV

ACTUALITY

1.   Since everything in this world is caused by the concurrence of causes and conditions, there can be no fundamental distinction between things.   The apparent distinctions exist because of people's absurd and deluding thoughts and desires.   In the sky there is no distinction of east and west; people create the distinction out of their own minds and then believe it to be true.   Mathematical numbers from one to infinity are each complete numbers, but each in itself carries no distinction of quantity; people

make the distinctions for their own convenience so as to be able to indicate varying amounts.

In the universal process of becoming, inherently there are no distinctions between the process of life and the process of destruction; people make a distinction and call the one birth and the other death. In action there is no distinction between right and wrong, but people make a distinction for their own silly convenience. Buddha keeps away from these distinctions and looks upon the world as upon a fleecy passing cloud. To Buddha every definitive thing is illusion, something that the mind constructs; he knows that whatever the mind can grasp and throw away are vanity; thus he avoids the pitfalls of images and discriminative thought.

2. People grasp after things for their own imagined convenience and comfort; they grasp after wealth and treasure and honors; they cling desperately to life; they make arbitrary distinctions between good and bad, right and wrong, and then vehemently affirm and deny them. For people life is a succession of graspings and attachments, and then, because of it, they must assume the illusions of pain and suffering.

Once there was a man on a long journey who came to a river. He said to himself; this side of the river is very difficult and dangerous, the other side seems easier and safer, but how shall I get across? So he builds himself a raft out of branches and reeds and safely crosses the river. Then he thinks to himself: This raft has been very useful

to me in crossing the river; I will not abandon it to rot
on the bank, but will carry it along with me; and thus he
voluntarily assumes an unnecessary burden.   Can this man
be called a wise man?   This parable teaches that a good
thing when it becomes an unnecessary burden should be
thrown away; how much more a bad thing.

A jar does not exist just because it is easily broken,
but knowing that the substance of a jar is not real, one
should not become attached to it, but if one gets rid of
the attachment, he can still use the jar, not to do so would
be an instance of throwing away something that, although
not perfect, is still useful.   We can speak of the horns
of a hare, of the child of a barren woman, but they never
exist.   To grasp after and to become attached to things
which have names but lack substance, is foolish.   Buddha
made it the rule of his life to avoid useless and unnecessary
discussions.

3.   It has been said that things do not come and do not
go, neither do they appear nor disappear, therefore, it is
wise not to become attached to things nor to lose things.
There are things that do not appear and do not disappear,
but they are different from that which is un-born and not
subject to destruction.

Buddha keeps away from both the affirmation of existence and the denial of existence; he preaches: It is both
nonexistence and not non-existence; it neither gives birth
to life, nor does it destroy life.   That is, everything being
a concordance and succession of causes and conditions,

a thing in itself does not exist, so it can be said it is non-existent.   At the same time, because it has a relative connection with causes and conditions, it can be said that it is not non-existent.

To adhere to a thing because of its form is the source of delusion.   If the form is not grasped and adhered to, this false imagination and absurd delusion will not occur. Enlightenment is the wisdom to see this truth and to avoid that foolish delusion.   The world, indeed, is like a dream and the treasures of the world are an alluring mirage! Like the apparent distances in a picture, things have no reality in themselves: they are like passing clouds.

4.   To believe that things created by an incalculable series of causes can last forever, is a serious mistake; but it is just as great a mistake to believe that things completely disappear.   These categories of everlasting life and everlasting death, and affirmation and denial of them, do not apply to the essential nature of things, but only to their appearances as they are observed by human eyes.   Because of human desire, people become related and attached to these appearances, but in their essential nature of things are free from all relations and attachments.

Since everything is created by a series of causes and conditions, the appearance of things is constantly changing; that is, there is no constancy about them as there should be about authentic substances.   It is because of this constant change of appearance that we liken things to a mirage and a dream.   But, in spite of this constant change in appearance, things, in their essential nature, are constant and changeless.   To illustrate:—A river to a man seems like a river, but to a hungry demon a river may seem to be like fire or ice.   Therefore, to speak to a man about a river existing or not existing would have some sense, but to this fabulous being, such words would have no meaning.   In like manner it can be said of everything: " Things are like illusions, they both exist and do not exist."

Further, it is a mistake to distinguish this passing life from a changeless life of truth.   It can not be said, that apart from this world of change and appearance, there is another world of constancy and truth.   This changing, passing life is the life of truth; there is but one authentic life.   But ignorant people of this world, assuming that this is a real world, proceed to act upon that absurd assumption.   But as this world is only an illusion, their acts being based upon error, only lead them into harm and suffering.   But a wise man, recognising that the world is but an illusion, does not act as if it was real, so he escapes the suffering.

V

THE MIDDLE WAY

1.   To those who choose the path that leads to Enlightenment, there are two extremes that should be carefully avoided:—First, there is the extreme of indulgence to the desires of the body, the whims of the mind and the pride

of life, that come naturally to those who cherish the notion that this world is a real world and this life an end in itself. Second, there is the opposite extreme that comes naturally to those who cherish the notion that a world of truth is the only reality; to them it comes easy to renounce this life and to go to an extreme of ascetic discipline and to torture one's body and mind unreasonably. The Noble Path that lies between these two extremes and leads to enlightenment and wisdom and peace of mind may be called the Life of Golden Mean. This Noble Path of the middle way, to which Buddha referred in the Four Noble Truths as leading to the extinction of desire and therefore to the ending of suffering, consists of eight stages: Right Ideas, Right Resolution, Right Speach, Right Behavior, Right Livelihood, Right Effort, Right Mindfulness, and Right Dhyana, or Concentration.

As has been said, all things appear or disappear by reason of an endless series of causes. Ignorant people see life as either existence, or non-existence, but wise men see beyond both existence and non-existence to something that includes them both; this is an observation of the Middle Way.

Suppose a log is floating in a river. If the log does not become grounded on either bank, or does not sink, or is not taken out by a man, or does not decay, ultimately it will reach the sea. Life is like this log caught in the current of a great river. If a person does not become attached to a life of self-indulgence, nor renouncing life become attached to a life of self-torture; if a person does not become proud of his virtue nor of his evil acts; if in his search for enlightenment he does not become contemptuous of delusion nor fear it; such a person is following the Middle Way by a Noble Path.

2.   The important thing in following the path to enlightenment, is to avoid being caught and entangled in any extreme; that is, to always follow a middle course. Knowing that things neither exist nor do not exist, remembering the dream-like nature of everything, reminding himself that even his supposed ego-personality has no substance of its own, one should avoid being caught by any desire for comfort, happiness, or success; or pride of personality, or praise for his good deeds, or caught and entangled by anything else.

But if one is to avoid being caught in the current of his desires, he must learn in the very beginning not to grasp after things lest he become habituated to them and become attached to them.   He must not become attached to existence nor to non-existence, to anything inside nor outside, neither to good things nor to bad things, neither to right nor wrong.   If he becomes attached to things, just at that moment, all at once, the life of delusion begins. The one who follows the Noble Path to Enlightenment will not cherish regrets neither will he cherish anticipations, but with equitable and peaceful mind will meet what comes.

3.   Enlightenment has no definite form or nature by

which it can manifest itself, so in enlightenment itself, there is nothing to be enlightened. Enlightenment exists solely because of delusion and ignorance, if they disappear so will enlightenment. And the opposite is true also: delusion and ignorance exist because of enlightenment; when enlightenment ceases, ignorance and delusion will cease also. Therefore, be on guard against thinking of enlightenment as a " thing " to be grasped after, lest it, too, becomes an obstruction. When the mind that was in darkness becomes enlightened, it passes away, and with its passing, the thing which we call enlightenment passes also.

As long as people desire enlightenment and grasp after it, it means that delusion is still with them; therefore, they who are following the way to enlightenment must not grasp after it, and if they gain enlightenment they must not become attached to it. When people attain enlightenment but still continue to cherish the notion of enlightenment, it means that enlightenment itself has become an obstructing delusion; therefore, people should follow the path to enlightenment until in their thoughts worldly passions and enlightenment become one thing.

4. This conception of universal oneness—that things in their essential nature have no distinguishing marks—is called " sunyata ". Sunyata means, the un-born, having no self-nature, no duality. It is because things in themselves have no form nor characteristics that we can speak of them as neither being born nor being destroyed. There

is nothing about the essential nature of things that can be described in terms of discrimination; that is why things are called, sunyata.

As has been pointed out, all things appear and disappear because of the concurrence of causes and conditions. Nothing ever exists entirely alone; everything is in relations to everything else. Wherever there is light there is shadow; wherever there is length, there is shortness; wherever, therefore, we assert self-substance, we must admit sunyata. As the self-nature of things can not exist alone, there must be emptiness. By the same reasoning, enlightenment can not exist apart from ignorance, nor ignorance apart from enlightenment. If things do not differ in their essence of nature, how can there be duality?

5. People habitually think of themselves as being connected with birth and death, but in reality there are no such conceptions. When people are able to realise this truth, they have realised the truths of non-duality and sunyata. It is because people cherish the idea of an ego-personality that they cling to the idea of possession, but since there is no such thing as an " ego," there can be no such thing as possession. As people are able to realise this truth, they will be able to realise the truth of no self-nature.

People cherish the distinction of purity and impurity, but in the nature of things there is no such distinction except as it rises from their false and absurd imaginations. In like manner people make a distinction between good and evil, but there is no good and no evil existing separately. People who are immersed in a world of social relations will make such a distinction, but those who are following the path to enlightenment should recognise no such duality, and it should lead them neither to praise the good and condemn the evil, nor to despise the good and condone the evil. People naturally fear calamity and long for good fortune, but if the distinction is carefully studied, calamity often turns out to be fortunate and good-fortune to be calamitous. The wise man learns to meet the changing circumstances of life with an equitable spirit, being neither elated by success nor depressed by failure. Thus one relises the truth of non-duality.

Therefore, all these words that express relations of duality—such as, existence and non-existence, worldly-passions and true-knowledge, purity and impurity, good and evil—all of these terms of contrast in one's thinking, as they lead only to confusion and delusion, should sedulously be avoided. As people keep free from such terms and from the motions engendered by them, by so much do they realise sunyata's universal emptiness.

6. Just as the pure and fragrant lotus grows out of the mud of a swamp rather than out of the clean loam of an upland field, so from the muck of worldly passions springs the pure enlightenment of Buddhahood. The absurd views of other schools and the delusions of worldly passions are, truly, the seed of Buddhahood.

If a diver is to secure his treasure of pearl he must

descend into the sea, braving all its dangers of jagged coral and vicious sharks, so one must face the perils of worldly passion if he is to secure the precious pearl of enlightenment.   He must first know suffering and loneliness before he will appreciate sympathy and compassion. One must first be lost among the mountainous crags of egoism and selfishness, before there will awaken in him the desire to find a path that will lead him to enlightenment.   There is a legend of a hermit of old who had such a desire to find the true path that he climbed a mountain of swords and threw himself into the fire and endured them because of his hope.   He who is willing to risk the perils of the path will find a cool breeze blowing on the sword-bristling mountains of selfishness and among the fires of hatred and, in the end, will come to realise that the selfishness and worldly passions against which he has struggled and suffered are enlightenment itself.

7.   If people adhere to one of two things, though it may appear to be good and right, there is antagonism of thought and, therefore, there is delusion.   It is a mistake for people to seek a thing supposed to be good and right, and to flee from another supposed to be bad and evil.   If people insist that all things are empty and transitory, it is just as great a mistake as it would be to insist that all things are real and do not change.   If people assert that everything is suffering, it is error; if they assert that everything is happiness, that is error, too.   If a person becomes attached to his ego-personality, it is a mistake, it cannot

save him from dissatisfaction and suffering; therefore the teaching of Buddha brings unity where before there has been opposing duality. If one believes there is no ego, it is also a mistake and it would be useless for him to practise the way of truth.

Buddha teaches the Middle Way where duality merges into oneness; a Noble Path that leads to contentment and peace.

CHAPTER THREE

BUDDHA NATURE

I

THE HUMAN MIND AND TRUE MIND

1. THE world is like a lotus pond filled with many different kinds of plants; there are blossoms of many different tints: some white, some pink, some blue, some red, some yellow; some grow under water, some spread their leaves on the water, and some raise their leaves above the water. Among men there are many more differences. There are differences of sex, but as for that there is no essential difference of nature, for women, with proper training, may attain enlightenment precisely as men. Among humans there are many kinds and degrees of mentality: some are wise some are foolish, some are good-natured some are bad tempered, some are easily led, some are difficult to lead, some possess pure minds and some have minds that are defiled; but these differences are negligible when it comes to the attainment of enlightenment.

To be a trainer of elephants, one must possess five qualifications: he must have good health, he must have confidence, he must have diligence, he must have sincerity of purpose, and he must have wisdom. To follow Buddha's Noble Path to enlightenment, one must have the

same five good qualities.   If one has these qualities, whether he be man or woman, it is possible to gain enlightenment; it need not take long to learn the Buddha's teaching, for all humans possess a nature that has affinity for
enlightenment.

2.   In the practice of the way to enlightenment, people
see the Buddha with their own eyes and believe in Buddha
with their own minds.   The eyes that see Buddha and the
mind that believes Buddha are the same eyes and the same
mind that, until that day, had wandered about in the
world of suffering.

   If a king is beset by bandits, before he attacks them,
he must find out where their camp is.   So when one is
beset by worldly passions, he should first find out their
seat.   If one is in a house when he opens his eyes he will
first notice the interior of the room and only later will he
see the view outside the window.   In like manner we cannot conceive the eye noticing external things before there
is coordination of the eye with the things within the house.

   If there is a mind within the body, it ought first to
know the things of the body, but generally people are
interested in external things and seem to know and care
little for the things within the body.   If the mind was
located outside the body, how could it keep in contact
with the needs of the body?   But, in fact, the body feels
what the mind knows, and the mind knows what the body
feels.   Therefore it can not be said that the human mind
is outside or independent of the body.   Then, where does

the mind exist?

3. From the beginning, people, being conditioned by their karma, have wandered about in ignorance being deluded by two fundamental things. First, they believed that the discriminating mind, which lies at the root of this life of birth and death, was their real nature; and, second, they did not know that, hidden behind the discriminating mind, they possessed a pure mind of enlightenment that was their true nature.

When a man closes his fist and raises his arm, the eye sees it and the mind discriminates it, but the mind that discriminates it is not the true mind. The discriminating mind is only a mind for the discrimination of imagined differences that greed and other moods relating to the self have created. The discriminating mind is subject to causes and conditions, it is empty of any self-substance, it is constantly changing. But since people believe that this mind is their real mind, the delusion enters into the causes and conditions that produce suffering.

The man opens his hand and the mind perceives it; but what is it that first moves? Is it the mind? or is it the hand? Or is it neither? No, if the hand moves, the moving mind is only a superficial appearance of mind; it is not true and fundamental mind.

4. Fundamentally everyone has a pure clean mind, but it is usually covered over by the defilement and dust of worldly desires which have arisen from his circumstances.

These worldly desires are not of the essence of his nature; they are something added, like intruders or guests in a home. The moon is often hidden by clouds, but its purity remains untarnished. Therefore, people must not be deluded into thinking that these worldly desires, whether they be guest or defilement, are their own true mind. They must continually remind themselves of this fact by continually awakening within themselves the pure and unchanging fundamental mind of enlightenment. As it is, being caught by changing worldly desires and being deluded by their own perverted ideas, they wander about in a world of delusion.

The disturbances and defilements of the human mind are aroused by greed and the reactions due to their changind circumstances. If the mind does not grasp and become attached to things as they pass, there will be no disturbed and defiled mind. The mind that is not disturbed by things as they occur, that remains pure and tranquil under all circumstances, is the true mind and should be the master.

We cannot say that an inn disappears just because the guest is out of sight, neither can we say that the true self has disappeared simply because a mind of changeable ideas and absurd views, which have been aroused by the changing circumstances of life, has temporarily hidden it from attention. No, the human mind, with its burden of false imaginations and its bonds of attachment that change with changing conditions, is not the fundamental and true nature of the human spirit.

5. Let us think of a lecture hall that is light while the sun is shining but is dark after the sun goes down. We can think of the light departing with the sun and the dark coming with the night, but we can not so think of the mind that perceives lightness and darkness. To whom does lightness and darkness belong that we may return them as to an owner? The mind that is susceptible to lightness and darkness can not be given back to anybody; it can only revert to its true nature which is the fundamental nature of the human spirit. It is only a temporary mind that momentarily notes changes of lightness and darkness as the sun rises and sets; it is only a temporary mind that has different feelings from moment to moment with the changing circumstances of life; it is not the real and true mind. The fundamental and true mind which realises the lightness and the darkness is the universal essence of mind.

The temporary feelings of good and evil, love and hatred, that have been aroused by surrounding and changing conditions, are only momentary reactions that have had their cause in the guests and the defilement accumulated by the human mind. Behind the desires and worldly passions which the mind entertains there abides, clear and undefiled, the fundamental and true essence of mind.

Water is round in a round receptacle and square in a square one, but water as water has no particular shape. People often forget this fact. People see this and that, they like this and dislike that, they discriminate existence from non-existence; and then being caught in these entanglements and becoming attached to them, suffer in consequence. If people would only give up their attachments to these imaginary and false discriminations, and would restore the purity of their fundamental minds, then both their true minds and their flesh would be free from defilement and suffering and would know the peacefulness that goes with that freedom.

II
THE MIND OF BUDDHA

1. We have spoken of the pure and true mind as being fundamental; it is also the seed of Buddhahood. We will explain this by a simile.

One can get fire if he holds a lense between the sun and some combustible, but where does the fire come from? The lense is an enormous distance from the sun; apparently there is no connection, but the fire certainly appears upon the combustible. But if the combustible was something that would not kindle, there would be no fire.

In like manner, if the light of Buddha's Wisdom is concentrated upon the human mind, its true nature which is Buddhahood will be enkindled, and its light will illumine the minds of other people by its brightness, and will awaken faith in Buddha. It is because of Buddha's mercy and compassion that he holds the lense of faith before all human minds that they may be enlightened.

2. Often people disregard the affinity of their true minds for Buddha's enlightened wisdom, and because of it are caught by the entanglement of worldly passions, and become attached to discriminations of good and evil, and then lament because of their bondage and suffering. Why is it the people, possessing this fundamental and pure mind, should still cling to false imaginations and doom themselves to wander about in a world of delusion and suffering, while all about them is the light of Buddha's wisdom?

Once upon a time a man looked into what he thought was the polished side of a mirror and not seeking his face became insane. How unnecessary it was for a man to become insane just because he had carelessly looked into the reverse side of a mirror! But it is just as foolish and unnecessary for a person to go on suffering because he does not gain enlightenment where he expects to find it. There is no failure in enlightenment; the failure is in people who for a long time have been seeking enlightenment in their discriminating and thinking minds, not realising that they are not true minds, but are imaginary minds that have been caused by the accumulation of greed and illusions overlaying and hiding their true mind. If the accumulation of false imaginations is cleared away, enlightenment will appear. But the strange thing is, that when people gain enlightenment they realise that without false imaginations there could be no enlightenment.

3. Buddha-nature is not something that comes to an end. Though wicked men should be born beasts, or hungry demons, or fall into hell, they can not lose their Buddha-nature. However buried in the defilement of flesh or concealed at the root of worldly desires and forgotten it may be, human affinity for Buddhahood is never quite extinguished.

There is an old story told of a man who fell into a drunken sleep. His friend stayed by him as long as he could but, being compelled to go and fearing that he might be in want, the friend hid a jewel in the drunken man's garment. When the drunken man recovered, not knowing that his friend had hid a jewel in his garment, he wandered about in poverty and hunger. A long time after the men met and the friend told the poor man about the jewel and advised him to search for it. Like the drunken man of the story, people wander about suffering in this life of birth and death, unconscious that hidden away in their inner nature, pure and untarnished, is the priceless treasure of Buddha-nature.

4. But however unconscious people may be of the fact that everyone has within his possession this supreme nature, and however degraded and ignorant they may be, Buddha never loses faith in them because he knows that in the least of them there are, potentially, all the virtues of Buddhahood. So Buddha preaches to them the Dharma, awakens faith in them, leads them away from their chimeras and teaches them that there is no difference between them-

selves and Buddhahood.

Buddha is one who has attained Buddhahood, people are those who are capable of attaining Buddhahood, that is all the difference there is between them.   But if anyone thinks that he has attained enlightenment, he is deceiving himself for, although he may be moving in that direction, he has not yet reached Buddhahood.   Buddha-nature does not appear without diligent and faithful effort, nor is the task finished until Buddhahood appears.

5.   Once upon a time a king gathered some blind men about an elephant and asked them to tell him what an elephant was like.   The first man felt of a tusk and said an elephant was like a giant carrot;   another happened to touch an ear and said he was like a great fan;   another touched his trunk and said he was like a pestle;   still another, who happened to feel of his leg, said he was like a mortar;   and another who grasped his tail, said he was like a rope.   Not one of them was able to tell the kind what was the real form of an elephant.

In like manner one might ask a hundred men to describe the nature of man and not one of them would be able to describe the true nature of a human being.   There is only one possible way by which the true nature of man, the nature that can not be disturbed by worldly desires nor destroyed by death, can be realised and that is by the Buddha's Noble Path and by those who practise it.

III

BUDDHA-NATURE AND EGOLESSNESS

1. We have been speaking of Buddha-nature as though it was something that could be described, as though it was similar to the " universal soul " of other teachings, which it is not. The concept of an " ego-soul " is something that has been imagined by a disturbed mind which has first grasped it and then has become attached to it, but which must be abandoned if one is to realise enlightenment. On the contrary Buddha-nature is something indescribable that must first be discovered before it can be realised. In one sense it resembles an " ego-personality " but it is not the " ego " that says " I " and " mine."

To believe in the existence of an ego is a negative belief, that thinks non existence is existence; to deny a universal nature would also be wrong for it would be thinking that existence was non-existence.

This can be explained in a parable. A mother took her sick child to a doctor. The doctor gave the sick child medicine and instructed the mother not to let the child nurse until the medicine was digested. The mother did not have the heart to refuse the child when it should try to nurse, so she anointed her breast with something bitter so that the child would keep away from her of its own account. After the medicine had had time to be digested the mother cleansed her breast and let the child nurse. The mother took this method of saving her child in kindness of heart for she loved the child.

Like the mother in the parable, Buddha, in order to remove misunderstandings and to break up attachments to an ego-self, denies the existence of an ego; and when the misunderstandings and attachments are done away with, then he explains the reality of the true mind that is Buddhahood. Attachment to an ego-self leads people into delusion, but faith in their Buddha-nature leads them to enlightenment. It is like the woman in a story who was bequeathed a chest and, not knowing that the chest contained gold, she continued to live in poverty, until another person opened the chest and showed her the gold. Buddha opens the minds of people and shows them the pure gold of their Buddha-nature.

2.   If people all have this Buddha-nature, why is there so much suffering from people cheating one another and killing one another? And why are there so many distinctions of rank and wealth, of rich and poor? Is it not because the Buddha-nature has been covered over by defilement and worldly passion and the delusion of their minds?

There is a story of a wrestler who was accustomed to wear as an ornament on his forehead a precious stone. One time when he was wrestling the stone was crushed into the flesh of his forehead. He thought he had lost the gem and went to a surgeon to have the wound dressed. When the surgeon came to dress the wound he found the gem embedded in the flesh and covered over with blood and dirt. He held up a mirror and showed the stone to the wrestler.

Buddha-nature is like the precious stone of this story: it becomes covered over by the dirt and dust of other interests and people think they have lost it, but often after many years some good teaching brings it to mind again. Buddha-nature exists in everyone no matter how deeply it may be covered over by greed, anger and foolishness, or buried by deeds and their retribution. But Buddha-nature can not be lost or destroyed; and because all other things are delusion, sooner or later it will reappear. Like the wrestler in the story who was shown the gem buried in flesh and blood by means of a mirror, so people are shown their Buddha-nature, buried beneath their desires and worldly passions, by means of the enlightenment of Buddha.

3. Buddha-nature is always pure and tranquil no matter how varied the temperaments and surroundings of people may be. Just as milk is always white regardless of the color of a cow's hide, so it matters not how differently karma may condition a person's life or what different effects may follow a person's acts and thoughts; Buddha-nature is always pure and the same.

There is a fable told in India of a magical medicine that was hidden in the snowy fastnesses of the Himalayas. For a long time men sought for it in vain, but at last a wise man located it by the sweetness of the water that was flowing from a water pipe. As long as the wise man lived he was able to get this medicine, but after his death the sweet elixir no longer appeared in the water but remained hidden in some far off spring in the mountains, and the water in the pipe turned sour and harmful and of different taste to every one who tried it.   In like manner Buddha-nature is hidden away beneath the wild growth of worldly passions and can rarely be discovered, but Buddha found it and revealed it to people, but as they receive it by their varying faculties it tastes differently to each other.

4.   The diamond is the hardest of known substances; sand and gravel can be ground to powder but diamonds remain unscratched.   Buddha-nature is like the diamond. Human nature, its body and mind will wear away but the nature of Buddhahood can not be destroyed.   The Buddha Dharma teaches that in human nature there may be endless varieties, but in Buddha-nature there is but one likeness, the likeness of Buddha.

Pure gold is procured by melting ore and removing all impure substances.   If people would melt the ore of their minds and remove all the impurities of worldly passion and egoism, they would all recover the same pure Buddha-nature.

CHAPTER FOUR

EVIL DESIRES

I

WORLDLY PASSIONS

1. THERE are two kinds of worldly passions that defile and cover-over the purity of Buddha-nature. The first is the passion for discrimination and discussion by reason of which people become confused in judgment. It may be called the delusion of reasoning. The second is the passion for emotional experience by reason of which people become confused as to values. This may be called the delusion of practice.

Both delusions of reasoning and delusions of practice at first seem fundamental but, really, there are two other worldly passions that are more fundamental. The first is ignorance, and the second is desire. The delusion of reasoning is based upon ignorance, and the delusion of practice is based upon desire, so that the two sets of worldly passion are really one set after all, and together they are the source of all wordly passions.

If persons are ignorant how can they reason correctly and safely? As people yield to desire, grasping, clinging and attachment inevitably follow. It is this constant grasping at every pleasant thing they see and hear that leads people into the delusions of practice. Why, some people even yield to the desire for the death of the body. From these primary sources all the worldly passions of greed, anger, foolishness, misunderstandings, and the infatuations of egoism, pride, deceit, jealousy, adulation, contempt, inebriety, selfishness, have their risings and appearings.

2.   Greed rises from wrong ideas as to what can give true satisfaction; anger rises from wrong ideas as to what is unsatisfactory in one's affairs and surroundings; foolishness rises from wrong ideas as to what one should do or should not do; misunderstandings arise from wrong ideas that follow listening to wrong teachings.

These three—greed, anger and foolishness—are called the fires of the world.   The fire of greed consumes those who have lost their true minds through greed; the fire of anger consumes those who have lost their true minds through anger; the fire of foolishness consumes those who have lost their true minds through their failure to hear and to heed the teachings of Buddha.   Indeed, this world is burning-up by its many and various fires.   There are fires of greed, fires of anger, fires of foolishness, fires of misunderstandings, fires of infatuation and egoism, fires of decrepitude, sickness and death, fires of sorrow, lamentation, suffering and agony.   Everywhere these fires are raging.   These fires of worldly passion not only burn the self, they cause others to suffer and they lead others into wrong acts of body, lips and mind.   From the wounds that are caused by these fires there issues a pus that infects and poisons every one it touches and leads them into evil paths.

3. Greed rises in the face of satisfaction; anger rises in the face of dissatisfaction; and foolishness rises from impure thoughts. The evil of greed has little impurity but is hard to remove; the evil of anger has more impurity but it is easy to remove; the evil of foolishness has much impurity and is very hard to overcome. Therefore, people should quench these fires whenever and wherever they appear, by rightly judging as to what can give true satisfaction, by strictly controlling the mind in the face of the unsatisfactory things of life, and by ever recalling Buddha's teachings of good-will and kindness. If the mind is filled with wise and pure and unselfish thoughts, there will be no place for worldly passions to take root.

4. Greed, anger and foolishness are like fever. If one gets this fever, even if he lie in a comfortable room, he will suffer and be tormented by sleeplessness. Those who have no such fever have no difficulty in sleeping peacefully, even on a winter night, on the ground and with only a thin covering of leaves, or on a hot summer's night in a crowded room.

These three—greed, anger and foolishness—are the source of all human woe. To get rid of these sources of woe, one must observe the moral precepts, he must practice concentration of mind and he must have wisdom. Observance of the moral precepts will remove the impur-

ities of greed; right concentration of mind will remove
the impurities of anger; and wisdom will remove the
impurities of foolishness.

5. Human desires are endless. It is like the thirst of a
man who drinks salt water: he gets no satisfaction and his
thirst is only increased. So it is with a man who seeks to
gratify his desires; he only gains increased dissatisfaction
and his woes are multiplied.

The gratification of desires never satisfies; it always
leaves behind an unrest and irritation that can never be
allayed, and then, if the gratification of his desires is
thwarted, it will often drive him insane. To satisfy their
desires, people will struggle and fight with each other,
king against king, vassal against vassal, parent against son,
older brother against a younger brother, sister against
sister, friend against friend, they will fight and even kill
each other to satisfy their desires.

People often ruin their lives in the attempt to satisfy
their desires. They will cheat and steal and oppress, and
then being caught will suffer from the disgrace of it and
its punishment. They will sin against their own flesh
knowing that the gratification will harm them. They
will sin against their own minds knowing perfectly well
that the gratification will ultimately bring unhappiness
and suffering, so imperious is desire.

And then there is karma and the suffering of following lives, and the agonies of falling into another world.

6. Of all the worldly passions, lust is the most intense. All other worldly passions seem to follow in its train. Lust seems to provide the soil in which other passions flourish. Lust is like a female demon that eats up all the good deeds of the world.

Lust is a viper hiding in a flower garden: it poisons those who come in search of beauty. Lust is a vine that climbs a tree and spreads over the branches until the tree is strangled. Lust insinuates its tentacles into human emotion and sucks away the good sense of the mind until the mind withers. Lust is a bait cast by the evil one that foolish people snap at and are dragged down into the depths of the evil world.

If a dry bone is smeared with blood a dog will gnaw at it until he is tired and baffled. Lust to a man is precisely like this bone to a dog, he will gnaw at it until he is exhausted. If a single piece of carrion is thrown to two wild beasts they will fight and claw each other to get it. If a foolish man carries a torch against the wind, he will likely burn himself. Like these two beasts and this foolish man, people fight and suffer because of worldly passion.

7. It is easy to shield the outer body from poisoned arrows, but it is impossible to shield the mind from the poisoned darts that originate within itself. Greed, anger, foolishness and the infatuations of egoism, these four poisoned darts originate within the mind and infect it with deadly poison. If people are infected with these poisons, they will lie, cheat, chatter, abuse, by words,

and then will actualise their words by killing, stealing and committing adultery. The three evil states of mind, the four evil words, and the three evil acts if added together become the ten gross evils.

If people become accustomed to lying, they will unconsciously commit wrong deeds. Before they can act evil they must lie, and once they begin to lie they will act evilly with unconcern.

But as these ten evils all originate within the mind, foolishness is the greatest of the worldly passions. So long as foolishness infects the mind, the mind will proceed to manifest its evil states in evil acts and unconcernedly. Greed, lust, fear, anger, egoism, misfortune, unhappiness, all have relation to foolishness. Thus, foolishness is the greatest of poisons.

8. From worldly passion action follows; from action suffering follows: passion, action, suffering are like a wheel rotating endlessly. The rolling of this wheel has no beginning and no ending, how can people escape rebirth? One life following another life according to its karmaic cycle in endless recurrence! If one were to pile the ashes and bones of men appearing in a karmaic cycle, the pile would be mountain high; if one were to collect the milk of mothers who have sukkled them, it would be deeper than the sea.

Although all people possess the nature of Buddhahood, it is buried so deeply in the defilement of worldly passion that it long remains unknown. That is why suffering is so universal and why there is this endless recurrence of lives of misery. But just as yielding to greed, anger and foolishness accumulates karma and conditions rebirth, so following Buddha's Dharma clears away the defilement of karma and ends re-birth in the world of suffering.

II
THE NATURE OF MAN

1. Man's nature is like a dense thicket that has no entrance into it and is difficult to penetrate. In comparison, the nature of an animal is much easier to understand. Still, if we cannot understand the nature of man perfectly, we can, in a general way, classify them according to outstanding differences.

First there are those who because of wrong teachings practise austerities and cause themselves to suffer. Second, there are those who, by cruelty, by stealing, and by other unkind acts, cause others to suffer. Third, there are those who cause other people to suffer but are willing to suffer with them; these are mostly social and political reformers. Fourth, there are those who do not suffer themselves and save others from suffering. This last class by following the teachings of Buddha do not give way to greed, anger and foolishness but live peaceful lives of kindness and wisdom.

2. There are other classifications. First, those who pass

from darkness to darkness; those that pass from darkness to light; those who pass from light to darkness; those who go from light to light.

Those who belong to the first group are born in unfortunate circumstances. They do not know about Buddha's teachings; their minds are clouded by ignorance, they act unwisely by wrong observation, and after death there is rebirth in this world of suffering. Those in the second group have heard of Buddha's teachings and, although born in poor circumstances, keep the mind pure, are sympathetic and charitable, and after death there is rebirth in this world but under better conditions. Those in the third group live in comfort and prosperity and, although they know of Buddha's teachings, do not follow them but give way to impure thoughts, are selfish, act unkindly, and after death there is return to this world of suffering. Those who belong to the fourth class, who go from light to light, live in contentment and comfort. They know and observe Buddha's teachings, they keep a pure mind, they are both charitable and sympathetic, they teach the Dharma to others; after death there is rebirth where there is no suffering.

3. Some men are like letters carved in a rock; they easily give way to anger and retain their angry thoughts for a long time. Some men are like letters written in sand; they give way to anger also, but the angry thoughts quickly pass away. Some men are like letters written in running water; they do not retain their passing thoughts, they

let abuse and uncomfortable gossip pass by unnoticed, their minds are always pure and undisturbed.

There are still other men: those who are proud, act rashly and are never satisfied; their nature is easy to understand. Then there are those who are courteous, who always act after consideration; their nature is hard to understand. Then there are those who have overcome desire completely; it is impossible to understand their nature.

Thus people can be classified in many different ways but their nature is hard to understand. Only Buddha understand them and by his wisdom leads them by many kinds of teaching.

III
THE LIFE OF MAN

1. There is an allegory that depicts human life. Once there was a man in a boat rowing down a river. A man on the shore warned him, saying, " Stop rowing so gaily down the swift current; there are rapids ahead and a dangerous whirlpool, and there are crocodiles and demons lying in wait in rocky caverns. You will perish if you persist." In this allegory, " the swift river " is a life of lust; " rowing gaily " is giving rein to one's passion; " rapids ahead " means the ensuing suffering and pain; " whirlpool " means, pleasure, " crocodiles and demons " refers to the decay and death that follows a life of lust and indulgence; " the man on shore," who calls out the

warning, is the Buddha.

Here is another allegory.   A man who has committed
a crime is running away; as guards are following him, he
tries to hide himself by descending into a well by means
of some vines that are growing in it.   As he descends he
notices a viper in the bottom of the well, so he decides to
cling to the vine for safety.   After a time when his arms
are getting tired, he notices two mice, a white one and a
black one, gnawing at the vine.   If the vine breaks, he
will fall on the viper and perish.   Suddenly, on looking
upward, he notices just above his face a bee-hive from
which occasionally falls a drop of honey.   The man, forgetting all his danger, tastes the honey with delight.

"A man" means those who are born to suffer and to
die alone.   "Guards" and "vipers" refer to the body
with all its desires.   "Vines in a well" means the con-
tinuity of the human life.   "Two mice, black and white"
refers to the duration of time, to night and day, and the
passing years.   "Sweet honey" is the rare happiness that
beguiles the suffering of the passing years.

2.   Here is still another allegory.   A king places four
vipers in a box and gives the box into the keeping of a
servant.   He commands the servant to take good care of
the serpents and warns him that if he angers them he will
be punished with death.   The servant, in fear, decides to
throw away the box and to escape himself.   The king
sends five guards to recapture the servant.   At first they
approach the servant in a friendly manner intending to

take him back safely, but the servant does not trust their
friendliness and escapes to another village.   Then in a
vision, a voice tells him that in this village there is no safe
shelter, and moreover there are six bandits who will attack
him, so the servant runs away in fright until he comes to
a wild river that blocks his way.   At first he is frightened
because of the dangers that are following him, but he
makes a raft and succeeds in crossing the turbulent current,
beyond which he finally finds safety and peace.

" Four vipers in a box " means the body of flesh made
up of the four elements of earth, water, fire and air.   The
body is given into the charge of the mind, but the body
is an enemy of the mind, and the mind tries to run away
from body.   " Five guards who approach in friendly
purpose " mean the five aggregates,—sensation, perception, imagination, karma and consciousness—which inform body and mind.   " The safe shelter " means the six
senses, which are no safe shelter after all, and " the six
bandits " are the six objects of desire of the six sense minds.
Thus, seeing the dangers within the six senses, he runs
away once more and comes to the wild current of worldly
desires.   Then he makes himself a raft of Buddha's good
teachings and crosses the wild current safely.

3.   There is a perilous place in a person's life called,
" leaving parents, leaving children "; there are three other
occasions that are full of peril when a son is helpless to
aid his mother or a mother help her son, namely, a conflagration, a flood and a burglary, yet even in these perilous

and sad occasions, there still exists a chance for aiding each other.   But there are another three occasions when it is impossible for a mother to save her son or a son to save his mother.   These three occasions are: the time of sickness, the time for growing old, and the hour of death.

How can a mother take her son's place when he is sick?   How can a son take her place when she is growing old?   How can either help the other when the hour of death approaches?   No matter how much they may love each other or how intimate they may have been, one cannot help the other on such occasions.   This is the real " parents leaving child, child leaving parents."

4.   Once Yama, the legendary King of Hell, asked a man who in life had acted very wickedly, whether, during his life, he had ever met the three heavenly messengers. The man replied: " No, my Lord, I never met any such persons."   Yama asked him, if he had ever met an old person bent with age and walking with a cane.   To this the man replied: " Yes, my Lord, I have met such persons frequently."   Then Yama said to him: " You are suffering this present punishment because you did not recognise in that old man a heavenly messenger sent to warn you that you must quickly change your ways before you too become an old man."

Yama asked him again, if he had ever seen a poor and friendless sick man.   The man replied: " Yes, my Lord, I have seen many such."   Then Yama said to him: " You have come into this place because you failed to

recognise in this sick man a messenger from heaven sent
to warn you of your own sickness."

Then Yama asked him once more, if he had ever seen
a dead man. The man replied: " Yes, my Lord, I have
been in the presence of death many times." Yama said
to him: " It is because you did not recognise in this dead
man a heavenly messenger sent to warn you, that you are
brought to this. If you had recognised this messenger and
taken his warning you would have changed your course,
and would not have come to this place of suffering."

5. Once there was a young woman named Kisagotami,
the wife of a wealthy man, who lost her mind because of
the death of her child. She took the child in her arms
and went from house to house begging people to heal her
child. Of course they could do nothing for her, but finally
a follower of Buddha advised her to see the Blessed One
who was then staying at the temple of Jetavana, so the
woman carried the dead child to Buddha.

The Blessed One looked upon her with sympathy and
said: " To heal the child I need some poppy seeds;
go and beg four or five poppy seeds from some home
where death has never entered." So the poor demented
woman went out and sought a house where death
had never entered but in vain and at last was obliged
to return to Buddha. In his quiet presence her mind
cleared and she understood the meaning of his words.
She took the body away and buried it and then returned
to Buddha and became one of his followers.

IV

ASPECTS OF HUMAN LIFE

1.   People in this world are prone to be selfish and un-
sympathetic; they do not know how to love and respect
each other; they argue and quarrel over trifling affairs to
their own harm and suffering, and life becomes only a
dreary round of unhappiness.

Regardless of whether they are rich or poor they
worry over money affairs; they suffer from poverty and
they suffer from wealth.   Because their lives are controlled
by greed, they are never contented and never satisfied.   A
wealthy man worries about his estate if he has one, he
worries about his mansion and its many servants, he worries about his health and comfort, he worries about his
treasures and their safety.   He worries lest some disaster
befall him, his mansion burn down, robbers break in,
bandits carry him off.   Then he worries about death and
the disposition of his wealth.   Indeed, his life is lonely,
and after death the future seems more lonely.

A poor man always suffers from insufficiency and this
serves to awaken endless desires, for land and house and
wealth and leisure and luxury.   Being aflame with greed
and covetousness he wears out both body and mind, and
comes to death in the middle of life.   The whole world
seems pitted against him and even the path after death
seems lonesome as though he had a long journey to go and
no friends to keep him company.

2. Then there are five evils in the world. First, there is cruelty; every creature even insects strive with one another. The strong attack the weak; the weak deceive the strong; everywhere there is fighting and cruelty. Second, there is no clear demarcation between the rights of a father and a son; between an elder brother and a younger; between a husband and a wife; between a senior relative and a younger; on every occasion each one desires to be the highest and to profit by the other. They cheat each other, there is double dealing and lack of sincerity. Third, there is no clear demarcation as to behavior between men and women. Everyone at times has impure and lascivious thoughts and desires that lead them into questionable acts and often into disputes and fightings and outright injustice and wickedness. Fourth, people are prone to disrespect the rights of others, they exaggerate their own importance at the expense of others, they set bad examples of behavior and are unjust in their speech, deceiving, slandering, abusing and using a double tongue. Fifth, people are prone to neglect their duties toward others. They think too much of their own comfort and their own desires; forget the favors they have received and they cause annoyance to others that often passes into gross injustice.

3. It is natural in this world of suffering for people to think and act selfishly and egoistically and because of it, it is equally natural for suffering and unhappiness to follow. It is natural for people to favor themselves and to neglect

others; it is natural for people to let their own desires run into greed and lust and all manner of evil; but because of it they must suffer endlessly.

These things are natural but are not absolute, for if people would listen to good teaching and do more considerate and careful thinking the suffering and unhappiness might be avoided.   Buddha has shown the world a safe path to enlightenment and emancipation; if people would believe in it and follow it all their suffering an unhappiness would be ended.

4.   Because this is a world of suffering people ought to have more sympathy for each other; they ought to respect each other for their good traits and help each other in their difficulties; but instead they are selfish and hard-hearted; they despise each other for their failings and dislike them for their advantages.   These aversions generally grow worse with time and after a while become intolerable.   Fortunately these feelings of dislike do not often eventuate in acts of violence but they poison life with feelings of hatred and anger that become so deeply carved into the mind that people carry the marks of it to the hour of death.

Truly, in this world of greed a man is born alone and dies alone, and there is no one to share his punishment in the life after death.   The law of cause and effect is universal; each man must carry his own burden of sin and must go alone to its retribution.   But, fortunately, the same law of cause and effect controls good deeds.   A life of sympathy and kindness will eventuate in good fortune and happiness.

5. Times of luxury do not last long, they pass away very quickly; nothing in the world can be long enjoyed.

Therefore people should cast away while they are young and healthy all their greed and attachment to worldly riches and affairs, and should seek earnestly for true enlightenment, for what lasting happiness can there be apart from enlightenment.

Most people, however, disbelieve or ignore this law of cause and effect. They go on in their habits of greed and selfishness oblivious of the fact that a good deed brings happiness and an evil deed brings misfortune. Nor do they really believe that one's acts in this life condition following lives and entail upon others the rewards and punishments of their sins. They lament and complain of their own sufferings entirely misunderstanding the significance of their present acts to following lives, and the relation of their sufferings to acts of previous lives. They think only of the present desire and the present suffering.

Nothing in the world is permanent or lasting, everything is changing and momentary and unpredictable. But people are ignorant and selfish and are concerned only with the desires and sufferings of the passing moment. They do not listen to good teachings nor do they try to understand them, they simply give themselves up to the present interest, like a wild dog or a wolf, and because they do not seek enlightenment there is no end to their own suffering nor to the sufferings of others.

6.   As the years go by and people see how strongly they are bound by greed and habit and suffering, they become very sad and discouraged.   Often in their discouragement they quarrel with others and sink deeper into sin and give up trying to do better; often their lives come to some untimely end in the very midst of their wickedness.   This falling into discouragement because of one's misfortunes and suffering is most unnatural and is contrary to the law of heaven and earth.   It is true that everything in this life is transitory and filled with uncertainty, but it is lamentable that anyone should ignore the fact and keep on trying to seek enjoyments and satisfaction of their desires.

7.   From beginningless time incalculable numbers of men have been born into this world of delusion and suffering, and they are still being born.   It is fortunate that the world has Buddha's teachings and that men can believe in them and be helped.

Because time of plenty do not last long and suffering is never far away, people should think deeply, should keep the mind pure and the body well, they should keep away from greed and evil and should seek the good.   To some people, fortunately, the knowledge of Buddha's teaching has come; they should seek to understand it and try to be born in Buddha's Pure Land.   Knowing Buddha's teachings, they should not follow others into greedy and sinful ways, nor should they keep Buddha's teachings to themselves, but they should follow Buddha's teachings and teach them to others.

CHAPTER FIVE

THE RELIEF OFFERED
BY BUDDHA

I

THE RELIEF OF BUDDHA

1. As already explained, people from beginningless ages have gone on yielding to their worldly passions, repeating sin after sin, and carrying a burden of into lerable acts, unable of their own wisdom or in their own strength to break these habits of greed and indulgence. If they are unable to overcome and remove worldly passions, how can they be expected to realise their true nature of Buddhahood?

Buddha, who perfectly understood human nature, had great sympathy for them and made a vow that he would do everything possible, even at the cost of great hardship to himself, to relieve them from their fears and suffering. To effect this relief he manifested himself as a Bodhisattva and uttered the following vows:—

(a) Though I enter Buddhahood, I shall not be satisfied until everybody in my country is sure of entering Buddhahood and gaining enlightenment.

(b) Though I enter Buddhahood, I shall not be satisfied unless my enlightening power reaches all over the world.

(c) Though I enter Buddhahood, I shall not be satisfied

unless my life-giving power endures through the ages
and saves innumerable people.

(d)   Though I enter Buddhahood, I shall not be satisfied
until all the Buddhas in the Ten Quarters unite in praising
my name.

(e)   Though I enter Buddhahood, I shall not be satisfied
unless people with sincere faith endeavor to be reborn in
my country, and unless people who repeat my name in
sincere faith even ten times actually succeed in doing so.

(f)   Though I attain Buddhahood, I will not be satisfied
until people everywhere determine to attain enlightenment,
determine to practise virtue, determine to be reborn in my
country, and utter these vows with sincerity.   To those
who do this I will appear at the hour of death with a great
company of Bodhisattvas to welcome them into my Pure
Land.

(g)   Though I attain Buddhahood, I will not be satisfied
until people everywhere, hearing my name, think of my
country and wish to be reborn there and, to that end, plant
seeds of virtue with sincerity, even though they are not
able to accomplish all their heart's desire.

(h)   Though I attain Buddhahood, I will not be satisfied
until all those who are reborn in my Pure Land are certain
to attain Buddhahood, so that they may lead many others
to enlightenment and to the practice of great compassion.

(i)   Though I attain Buddhahood, I will not be satisfied
until people all over the world are influenced by my spirit
of loving compassion that will purify their minds and heal
their bodies and lift them above the things of the world.

(j)   Though I attain Buddhahood, I will not be satisfied until people everywhere, hearing my name, gain right ideas about life and death, and gain that perfect wisdom that will keep their minds pure and tranquil in the midst of the world's greed and suffering.

Thus I utter these vows; may I not gain Buddhahood until they are fulfilled.   May I become the source of unlimited Light, freeing and radiating the treasures of Wisdom and Virtue, enlightening all lands and emancipating all suffering people.

2.   Thus Buddha, by accumulating innumerable virtues through many æons of ages, became the Buddha of Infinite Light and Boundless Life and perfected his own Buddhaland of Purity wherein he is now living in a world of Peace teaching all people by his own spirit.

This Pure Land, wherein there is no suffering, is, indeed, most peaceful and happy.   Clothing, food and all beautiful things appear as those who live there wish for them.   When a gentle breeze passes through its jewel-laden trees, the music of its holy teachings fills the air and cleanses the minds of all who listen to it from all impurity. In this Pure Land there are many fragrant lotus blossoms, and each bloom has many precious petals, and each petal shines softly in unspeakable beauty.   The radiance of these lotus blossoms brightens the path of Wisdom, and those who listen to the music of the holy teaching are led by that path into perfect peace.

3.   Now all the Buddhas of the Ten Quarters, each in his own Buddha-land, are praising the virtues of this Buddha of Infinite Light and Boundless Life.   Whoever in these many Buddha-lands hears this Buddha's Name magnified and receives it with joy, his mind becomes one with Buddha's mind and he will be reborn in Buddha's wondrous Land of Purity.   Those who are born in that Pure Land share in Buddha's boundless life; their hearts are immediately filled with sympathy for all sufferers and at once they utter their own vows and go forward to manifest Buddha's method of relief.

In the spirit of these vows they cast away all worldly adherence and devote their merits to the emancipation of all sentient life; they integrate their own lives with the lives of all others, sharing their illusions and sufferings but, at the same time, realising their freedom from the bonds and attachments of the worldly life.   They know the hindrances and difficulties of the worldly life but they know, also, the boundless potentialities of Buddha's mercy.   They are free to go or come, they are free to advance or to stop as they wish, but they choose to remain with those upon whom Buddha has compassion.

Therefore, if anyone hearing the Name of this Buddha of Infinite Light is encouraged to call upon that Name in perfect faith, he shall share in Buddha's mercy.   So all people should listen to Buddha's teaching and should follow it even if it seems to lead them again through the flames that envelope this world of life and death.   If people truly and earnestly wish to gain enlightenment,

they must rely on Buddha.   It is impossible for an ordinary person to realise his supreme Buddha-nature without the support of Buddha.

4.   Buddha is not far from anyone.   His Land of Purity
is described as being far away in the Western Quarter but
it is, also, within the minds of those who are earnestly
devoted to the attainment of Buddhahood.   As people
picture in their minds the figure of Buddha it is shining
in golden splendor but, as they look at it, it divides into
eidhty-four thousand figures and each figure is emitting
eighty-four thousand rays of light and each ray of light
enlightens a world, never leaving in darkness a single
person who is reciting the name of Buddha.   Thus Buddha
helps people to take advantage of the relief he offers.

By seeing the image of Buddha, one is enabled to
realise the mind of Buddha.   The Buddha's mind is a
great compassion that includes all, even those who are
ignorant of his mercy or forgetful of it, much more those
who remember it in faith.   To those who have faith he
offers opportunity to become one with him.   As Buddha
is the all-inclusive body of compensation, whoever thinks
of Buddha, Buddha thinks of him and enters his mind
freely.   This means, that when a person thinks of Buddha,
he has Buddha's mind in all its pure and happy and peaceful
perfection.   In other words, he is Buddha.   Therefore,
each one in purity and sincerity of faith, should picture his
own mind as being Buddha's mind.

5. Buddha has many forms of transformation and incarnation, and can manifest himself in manifold ways according to the skilful means his wisdom and compassion indicate. Sometimes he can demonstrate his body in immense size to cover all the sky and stretch away into the boundless stellar spaces. Sometimes he manifests in the infinitesimals of nature, sometimes in forms, sometimes in energy, sometimes in aspects of mind, and sometimes in personality.

But in some manner or other he will surely appear to those who recite the name of Buddha in faith. To such he always appears accompanied by two Bodhisattvas, the Bodhisattva of Mercy and the Bodhisattva of Wisdom. His manifestations fill all the world for everyone to see but only those who have faith notice them. Those whose faith has been awakened and quickened by their vows are enabled to see his temporal manifestations which bring them abiding satisfaction and happiness, but those whose karma and faith enable them to see the real Buddha, are able to realise incalculable fortunes of joy and peace.

6. The Mind of Buddhahood with all its boundless potentialities of love and wisdom is compassion itself; Buddha can save anyone. Even the most wicked of people, those who commit unbelievable crimes; whose minds are filled with greed, anger and infatuation; those who lie, chatter, abuse and cheat, with lips; those who steal and act lasciviously; those who are near the end of their lives after years of evil deeds; even those who are already

destined to long ages of punishment; even these and all of them.   If a good friend comes to them and pleads with them, saying, "You are now facing death, you cannot blot out your life of wickedness, but you can take refuge in the compassion of the Buddha of Infinite Light."

In his suffering the wicked man can not understand all about Buddha, but he can repeat the words, "Adoration to Amida Buddha," and by repeating the holy name in singleness of mind, all the sins which have led him into baffling delusions will be cleared away.   If simply repeating the holy name can do this, how much more if one is able also to think about Buddha.   These who are thus able to repeat the holy name, when they come to the end of life, will be met by Amida Buddha and the Bodhisattvas of Mercy and Wisdom and will be led by them into Buddha's Land, where they will be reborn in all the purity of the white lotus.   Therefore, everyone should keep in mind the words, Adoration to Amida Buddha!

II

BUDDHA'S LAND OF PURITY

1. The Buddha of Boundless Life and Infinite Light is ever living and is ever radiating his Dharma.   In his fair Land there is no suffering and no darkness, and every hour is passed in joy, therefore, it is called the Land of joy.

In the midst of this Land there is a lake of pure water, fresh and sparkling, whose waves lap softly on shores of golden sands.   Here and there, there are lotus blossoms of many and various tints and colors, whose fragrance fills the air. At different places on the margin of the lake there are pavilions decorated with gold and silver, lapis lazuli and crystal, with marble steps leading down to the water's edge. At other places there are parapets and balustrades overhanging the water and enclosed with curtains and networks of precious gems, and in between there are groves of spice trees and flowering shrubs.

The earth is luminous with beauty and the air is vibrant with celestial harmonies. Six times during the day and night, delicately tinted flower petals fall from the sky and people gather them and carry them instantly to all the other Buddha-lands and make offerings of them to the myriad Buddhas, and are back again in Amida's Pure Land with the speed of thought.

2.   In this wondrous Land there are many birds and there are no birds of evil omen. There are snow-white storks and swans, and gay-colored peacocks and tropical birds of paradise, and flocks of little birds, softly twittering; and all these birds are birds of transformation. In Buddha's Pure Land they are sweetly singing birds, but in the land of birth and death they are voicing Buddha's teachings and praising Buddha's virtues. Whoever hears and listens to the music of these voices, listens to Buddha's voice and awakens to a newness of faith, joy and peace, in fellowship with the brotherhood of disciples everywhere.

Soft zephyrs pass through the trees of that Pure Land and stir the fragrant curtains of the pavilions and pass away in sweet cadences of music. People hearing faint echoes of this heavenly music think of Buddha, of the Dharma, of the fellowship of believers. All these excellencies are but reflections of the common things of the Pure Land.

3. Why is Buddha called, the Buddha of Infinite Light and the Buddha of Boundless Life? It is because the splendor of his Truth radiates unimpeded to the outermost and to the inmost limits of the Buddha-lands, it is because the vitality of his living compassion never wanes through asamkhyas of kaplas of lives and aeons of time. It is because those who are reborn in his Pure Land are perfectly enlightened and will never again return to the world of delusion and death.

It is because the number of those who by his Light are awakened into newness of Life is incalculable. Therefore, should all people concentrate their minds on the Divine Name and, as they come toward the end of life even for seven days or one day, they should recite the Buddha's Name in perfect faith. If they do this with undistracted mind they will be reborn in Buddha's Land of Purity and when he is reborn in the Pure Land he will be met and welcomed by all the Buddhas.

If any man hearing of Buddha's Name, awakens faith in his Dharma, concentrates his mind on Buddha, he will be guided and supported by all the Buddhas and Bodhisattvas until he attain perfect enlightenment.

SECTION THREE

THE WAY OF PRACTICE

CHAPTER ONE

THE WAY OF PURIFICATION

I

PURIFICATION OF MIND

1. PEOPLE have worldly passions which lead them into delusions and suffering. There are five ways of emancipation from the bonds of worldly passion.

First, they should have right ideas of things, ideas that are based on careful observation and true understanding of causes and effects and their significance. Since the cause of suffering is seated in the mind's desire and attachment, and since desire and attachment is related to wrong observations of an ego-self and neglect of the significance of the law of cause and effect, and since it is from these wrong obersvations and neglect that the worldly passions arise, there can be peaceful circumstances if the mind can be rid of these wrong observations.

Second, people can get rid of these wrong observations and following worldly passions, by careful and patient mind-control. With efficient mind-control they can avoid desires arising from the sensations of the eyes, ears, nose, tongue, body and the mental processes and, by so doing, will prevent all worldly passions from arising.

Third, they should have correct ideas in regard to the proper use of all things. That is, in regard to articles of food and clothing, they should not think of them in relation to comfort and pleasure, but only in their relation to the body's needs.   Clothing is necessary to protect the body against extremes of heat and cold, and to conceal the shame of the body; food is necessary for the nourishment of the body while it is training for enlightenment and Buddhahood.   Worldly passions do not arise from the necessary use of these things.

Fourth, people should learn endurance; they should learn to endure the discomforts of heat and cold, hunger and thirst; they should learn to be patient when receiving abuse and scorn; for it is the practice of endurance that quenches the fire of worldly passion which is burning up their bodies.

Fifth, people should learn to avoid all danger.   Just as a wise man keeps away from wild horses or mad dogs, so a man should not make friends with evil men, nor should he go to places that wise men avoid.   If one practises caution and prudence the fire of worldly passion which is burning at their vitals will die down.

2.   There are five groups of desires in the world that are to be avoided.   Desires arising from the forms the eyes see; from the sounds the ears hear; from the fragrance the nose smells; from tastes pleasant to the tongue; from things that are agreeable to the sense of touch; from these five groups of desires come the body's love of comfort. Most people being influenced by the body's love of comfort do not notice the evils that follow comfort, and they

are caught in a trap like a deer in the forest that is caught in a hunter's trap. Indeed, these five groups of desires arising from the senses are most dangerous traps. Being caught by them, people are entangled in worldly passions and it is not easy to get free from them.

3. There is no one way to get free from the traps of worldly passion. Suppose you had caught a snake, a crocodile, a bird, a dog, a fox and a monkey, six creatures of very different nature, suppose you tie them together with a strong rope and let them go. These six creatures will each try to go back to its own lair by its own method: —the snake will seek a covering of grass, the crocodile will seek water, the bird will want to fly in the air, the dog will seek a village, the fox will seek the solitary ledges, and the monkey will seek the trees of the forest. In the attempt of each to go his own way there will be a struggle but, being tied together by a rope, the strongest will drag the rest.

Like the animals in this example, man is tempted in different ways by the desires of his six senses, eyes, ears, nose, tongue, touch and mind, and is controlled by the predominant desire. Each group of desires at first tries to have its own way but being tied together in one organism they must ultimately move together. But if the six creatures are all tied to a post, after trying to get free until they are all tired out, they will all lie down at the post. Now mind is the strongest and is always the master. If people will train and control the mind there will be no further trouble from the other five senses. If the mind is under control people will get happiness both now and in the future.

4.   But it is not safe to trust the mind to run wild. Just as the other senses love beautiful and agreeable things, so the mind loves its egoistic comfort which is the love of fame and praise. But fame and praise are like incense that consumes itself and soon disappears. If people chase after honors and public acclaim and forget to keep their deeds right, they are in serious danger and will soon have cause for regret.

To chase after fame and wealth and power and love-affairs is like a child licking honey from the blade of a knife. It is like carrying a torch against a high wind, the flame will burn his own hands and face. One can not trust a mind that is filled with greed, anger and infatuation. One must not let the mind run free, it must be kept under strict control.

5.   To attain perfect mind-control is a most difficult thing to do. Those who seek to gain enlightenment must first get rid of all mental desires. Desire is a raging fire and if one is seeking enlightenment he must keep away from desire as a man would keep away from sparks if he was carrying a load of hay on his back.

But it would be foolish for a man to put out his eyes just because he is fearful of being tempted by beautiful forms; it is foolish to blind oneself and give the mind license. The mind is master and if the mind is under control, lesser desires will disappear. It is difficult to find the way to enlightenment, but it is more painful if people have no mind to seek such a way. Without enlightenment there is endless suffering in this world of life and death.

Seeking for the way to enlightenment is like an ox carrying a heavy load through a field of mud. When an ox is tired he can stop and rest, but the mud of greed is too deep for the mind to rest. But if the mind is controlled and kept on the right path there will be no mud of greed to hinder and all its suffering will disappear.

6. Those who seek a sure path to enlightenment must first remove all egoistic pride and be humbly willing to become disciples. The cost will be heavy but all the treasure of the world, all its gold and silver and honors, are not to be compared with wisdom and virtue. To be able to enojy good health, to bring true happiness to one's family, to bring a sense of peacefulness to everybody, one must first discipline and control his own mind. If he can control his mind he can find the way of enlightenment and all wisdom and virtue will naturally come to him.

Just as treasures are uncovered from the earth, so virtue appears from good deeds, and wisdom appears from a pure and peaceful mind. To walk safely through the maze of human life, one needs the light of wisdom and the guidance of virtue. The Buddha's teaching, which tells people how to get rid of greed, anger and infatuation, is a good teaching and those who follow it attain the happiness of a good life.

7.   Human beings tend to move in the direction of their thoughts.   If they harbor greedy thoughts, they become more greedy; if they think angry thoughts, they become more angry; if they cherish thoughts of revenge, their feet move in that direction.

In harvest time farmers keep their flock confined, lest they break through the fences into the harvest field and give cause for complaint or retaliation; so people must closely guard their minds against trespass and misfortune.   They must get rid of the thoughts that stimulate greed, anger and infatuation, and encourage thoughts that stimulate greed and evil deeds.

When spring comes and the pastures have an abundance of green grass, the farmers turn their cattle into the pastures but even then they keep a close watch over them. It is even so with the mind: under the best of conditions the mind will bear watching.

8.   In mind control patience and perseverance are essential.   At one time the Blessed One was staying at the town of Kausambi.   In this town there was one who cherished hard feelings toward him and who bribed wicked men to circulate false stories about him.   Under these circumstances it was difficult for the disciples to get sufficient food from their begging and there was plenty of abuse.

Ananda said to the Blessed One: " We had better

not stay in a town like this; there are other and better towns to go to; we had better leave this town."

The Blessed One replied: " Supposing the next town is like this, what shall we do? "

" Then we can go to another."

The Blessed One replied: " No, Ananda, there will be abuse wherever we go. We had better remain here and bear the abuse patiently until it ceases, then we can go to another place. Many things must be taken into consideration besides abuse. There are profits and losses, slander and honor, praise and abuse, suffering and pleasures; Buddha is not controlled by these external things, they will cease as quickly as they came."

II

THE WAY OF BEHAVIOR

1. Those who are seeking the way of enlightenment must always bear in mind the necessity of constantly keeping pure their body, lips and mind. To keep the body pure one must not kill any living creature, one must not steal, nor act immorally. To keep the lips pure, one must not lie, nor abuse, nor deceive, nor indulge in idle chatter. To keep the mind pure one must remove all greed and anger and false judgment.

If the mind becomes impure, the following deeds will be impure; if the deeds are impure, there will be mental suffering, so it is of the greatest importance that the mind be kept pure.

2.   Once there was a rich widow who had a good reputation for kindness, modesty and courtesy.   She had a housemaid who was wise and diligent.   One day the maid thought: " My mistress has a very good reputation; I wonder whether she is good by nature, or is good because of her surroundings.   I will try her and find out."

The following morning the maid did not appear before her mistress until nearly noon.   The mistress was vexed and scolded her impatiently.   The maid replied:

" If I am lazy for only a day or two, you ought not to become impatient."   Then the mistress became angry. The following day the maid was late again.   This made the mistress very angry and she struck the maid.   This incident became known and the rich widow lost her good reputation.

3.   Many people are like this woman.   While surroundings are satisfactory they are kind, modest and quiet, but when conditions change and are unsatisfactory, then they are otherwise.   We can not call a person really good who only has a peaceful mind and acts rightly when his surroundings are satisfactory.   It is only when a person maintains a pure and peaceful mind and whose acts continue good when unpleasant words enter their ears and when other people show ill-will toward them, or when they lack sufficient food, clothes and shelter, that we may call them good.   As it is only those who have received the Buddha's teaching and who have trained their minds

and bodies by those teachings who can manifest these virtues in the face of unpleasant and unsatisfactory things of life, it is only they who can be called really good and modest and peaceful people.

4. As to purity by words.   There are five pairs of words that cause much disturbance in the world:—words that are suitable on some occasions and wrong on other occasions; words that fit certain facts and words that do not fit the facts; some words are quieting, some are wild; some words are beneficial, some harmful; some words are sympathetic, some are hateful.   Whatever words we utter should be chosen with care for people will hear them and be influenced by them for good or ill.   If our minds are filled with sympathy and compassion, they will be resistent to the evil words we hear, and we must not let wild words pass our lips lest they arouse feelings of anger and hatred.   The words we speak should always be words of sympathy and wisdom.

Suppose there is a man who wants to remove all the dirt from the ground.   He uses a spade and a winnower and works perseveringly scattering the dirt all about, but in vain.   Like this foolish man we can not hope to get rid of all words but we can train our minds and fill them with sympathy so that other minds will be undisturbed by the words they hear.

One might like to paint a picture with water colors on the blue sky, but it is impossible.   So it is impossible to dry up a great river by the heat of a torch made of hay;

or to produce a crackling noise by rubbing together two pieces of well-tanned leather.   Like these examples, people should train their minds to be resistent to the words they hear.   They should train their minds and keep their minds broad as the earth, unlimited as the sky, deep like a river and soft as well-tanned leather.

Even if your enemy catches you and tortures you, if you have feelings of resentment, you are not following the Buddha's teachings.   Under every circumstance you should learn to think:—" My mind is resistent.   Words of hatred and anger shall not pass my lips.   I will surround such people with thoughts of sympathy and pity overflowing from a mind filled with compassion for all animate life."

5.   There is a fable told of a man who found an anthill which burnt in the daytime and smoked at night.   He went to a wise man and asked his advice as to what he should do about it.   The wise man told him to dig into it with a sword.   This the man did.

First he found a gate-bar, then some bubbles, then a pitchfork, then a box, a tortoise, a butcher-knife, a piece of meat and, finally, a dragon came out.   The man reported to the wise man what he had found.   The wise man explained the significance of it.   He said, " Throw away everything but the dragon.   Let the dragon alone.   Worship the dragon."

This is only a fable in which " anthill " represents the human body.   " Burns in the daytime " represents the fact that during the day time people turn into acts the things they thought about during the previous night. " Smokes in the night " indicates the fact that people during the night recall with pleasure or regret the things they had done during the previous day. "A man " means a person who notices things and seeks enlightenment. "A wise man " means Buddha. "A sword " means pure wisdom. " Dig into it " refers to the effort he must make to gain enlightenment. " Gate-bar " represents ignorance, " bubbles " are puffs of suffering and anger, " pitchfork " suggests hesitation and uneasiness, " box " suggests the storage of greed, anger, laziness, fickleness, repentance and regret; " tortoise " means the mind, " butcher-knife " means the synthesis of the five sense desires, and " piece of meat " means the resulting desire that causes a man to grasp after satisfaction. These things are all harmful to a man, so Buddha said, " throw them away."

" Dragon " means a mind that has put away all worldly passion. If a man digs into the things about him with the sword of wisdom he will finally come to this dragon. " Leave this dragon alone; do not disturb him; worship the dragon."

6. Pindola, a disciple of Buddha, after gaining enlightenment returned to Kausambi, his native place, to repay them for the kindness they had shown him. By so doing he prepared the field for later sowing Buddha-seeds.

On the outskirts of Kausambi city there is a small

park that runs along the bank of the river Ganga, that is
shaded by many cocoanut trees and where a cool wind
blows unceasingly.   One day in summer, the Lord Udana
came to this park with his consorts for recreation and,
after music and pleasure, he fell asleep in the shade of a
tree.   His wives and ladies-in-waiting, while their Lord
was asleep, took a walk and suddenly came upon Pindola
sitting in meditation in the shade of another tree.   They
recognised him as a holy-man and asked him to teach
them, which he did.

When the Lord awoke from his sleep, he went in
search of his ladies and found them surrounding and listening to this man.   Being of a jealous and lascivious mind,
the Lord became angry and abused Pindola, saying: " It
is inexcusable that you, a holy-man, should be in the
midst of women and talking with them," Pindola quietly
closed his eyes and remained silent.

The angry Lord drew his sword and threatened
Pindola, but Pindola remained silent.   This made the
Lord still more angry and he broke open an anthill and
threw some of the ant-filled dust upon him, but still
Pindola remained silent and quietly endured the insult and
pain.   Then the Lord became ashamed of his angry conduct and begged Pindola's pardon.   As a result of this
incident Buddha's teaching found its way into the Lord's
castle and from there it spread all over the country.

7.   A few days later the Lord Udana visited Pindola in
the forest retreat where he lived and asked him, saying:—

" Honored teacher, how is it that disciples of the Buddha can keep their bodies and minds pure and untempted by lust, although they are mostly young men? Pindola replied:—" Noble Lord, the Blessed One has taught us to respect all women. He has taught us to look upon all old women as our mothers, upon those of our own age as sisters, upon younger ones as our daughters. Because of this teaching the disciples of Buddha able to keep their bodies and minds pure and untempted by lust although they are youthful."

The Lord continued:—" But, Honored teacher, one may have impure thoughts of a woman even though he consider her as a mother, or a sister, or a daughter. How do the disciples of Buddha control their thoughts? "

" Noble Lord, the Blessed One taught us to think of our bodies as secreting impurities of all kinds, blood, pus, sweat and fats, by thinking thus we are able to keep our minds pure."

" Honored teacher," still pressed the Lord, " It may be easy for you to do this for you have trained your bodies and minds, but it would be difficult for those who have not had training. They may try to think impurities but their eyes will follow beautiful forms. They may try to see ugliness but they will be tempted by the beautiful figures just the same. There must be some other reason that the young men among the Buddha's disciples are able to keep their actions pure."

" Noble Lord," replied Pindola, " the Blessed One teaches us to watch the doors of the five senses. When

we see beautiful figures and colors with our eyes, when
we hear pleasant sounds with our ears, when we smell
fragrance with our nose, or when we taste sweet things
with our tongue, or touch soft things with our hands,
we are not to become attached to these attractive things,
neither are we to be repulsed by unattractive things.   It
is by this teaching of the Blessed One, to keep a constant
watch at the door of the senses, that the young disciples
are able to keep their minds and bodies pure."

" The teaching of the Blessed One is truly marvelous.
From my own experience I know that if I confront anything beautiful or pleasing without being on my guard,
I am disturbed by the sense impressions.   It is of vital
importance that one be on guard at the door of the senses,
at all times."

8.   Whenever a person expresses the thoughts of his mind
in action there is always a reaction that follows.   If one
abuses you, there is a temptation to answer in kind, or to
become revenged.   One should be on guard against this
natural reaction.   It is like spitting in the wind, it harms
no one but the self.   It is like sweeping dust against the
wind, it does not get rid of the dust but it defiles oneself.
Misfortune always dogs the steps of one who gives way
to the desire for revenge.

The same is true of pleasant acts:—if one makes a
present there is a natural desire to expect something in
return, or if one receives a present or a kindness there is
an impulse to return something similar.   There is really

more danger in the reaction to pleasant things than to evil things, because one is tempted to please the other regardless of the wisdom of the act. For instance, there is pleasure in music and entertainments and dancing; in themselves they seem harmless, but in their reactions there are evils against which one should be on guard. Music after all is only an exciting of the emotions, and the dance is but the act of a crazy mind to cover the desire for something quite different. Those who seek enlightenment can well afford to avoid the allurements of music and dancing; and those who are seeking to realise a quiet mind should avoid entertainments and only smile when they face something pleasant.

9.   Better than a selfish mind that desires and seeks after pleasant things for oneself, is a mind intent on following the Noble Path. One should get rid of a selfish mind and replace it with a mind that is earnest to help others. An act to make another happy, inspires the other to make still another happy, and so happiness is aroused and abounds. Thousands of candles can be lighted from a single candle, and the life of the single candle will not be shortened. Happiness never decreases by being shared.

Those who seek enlightenment must be careful of their first steps. No matter how high one's aspiration may be, it must be attained step by step, and first steps must be taken first. The first steps on the path to enlightenment must be taken in our every-day life, today and tomorrow and the next day.

10. At the very beginning of the path to enlightenment there are twenty difficulties. 1. It is hard for a poor man to be very generous. 2. It is hard for a rich man to learn the way of enlightenment. 3. It is hard to seek enlightenment at the cost of self-sacrifice. 4. It is hard to see the Buddha-world in the present world. 5. It is hard to hear the Buddha-teaching in the turmoil of the world's life. 6. It is hard to keep the mind pure against the instincts of the body. 7. It is hard not to desire things that are beautiful and attractive. 8. It is hard for a strong man not to use his strength to satisfy his desires. 9. It is hard when one is insulted not to get angry. 10. It is hard to remain innocent when tempted by sudden circumstances. 11. It is hard to apply oneself to study. 12. It is hard not to despise a beginner. 13. If successful it is hard to keep humble. 14. It is hard to get a good friend. 15. It is hard to endure the discipline that leads to enlightenment. 16. It is hard not to be disturbed by external conditions and circumstances. 17. It is hard to teach others by being mindful of their natures. 18. It is hard to attain a peaceful mind. 19. It is hard not to argue about right and wrong. 20. It is hard to find and learn and practise a good method.

11. Good men and bad men differ from each other in three characteristics. Bad men do not recognise a sinful act to be sinful; if the sinfulness of the act is brought to their attention, they do not cease doing it, they do not

like to have anyone inform them of their sinful acts.

Wise men are sensitive to right and wrong; wise men cease doing anything as soon as they see that it is wrong; wise men are grateful to anyone who calls their attention to wrong acts.

Thus good men and bad men differ radically. Bad men never appreciate kindnesses shown them, but wise men appreciate and are grateful. Wise men try to express their appreciation and gratitude by some return of kindness, not only to their benefactor, but to everyone else.

III

TEACHING BY ANCIENT FABLES

Many of the Buddha's teachings were uttered in the form of parables and fables, some of which, no doubt, were in circulation long before his day. At first they seem out of place in modern thought, but as they enshrine profound truths some of them are repeated here.

1. Once upon a time there was a country which had the very peculiar custom of abandoning its aged people in remote and inaccessible mountains. A certain good man found it very difficult to follow this custom in the case of his aged father, so he built a secret underground cave where he hid his father and cared for him.

One day a god appeared before the king of that country and asked him a puzzling question, saying that if he could not answer it satifsactorily, his country would be destroyed. Here is the question: " Here are two serpents; tell me the sex of each."

Neither the king nor anyone in the palace was able to answer the question; so the king offered a reward to anyone in his kingdom who would solve the problem. The good man went to his father's hiding place and asked him. The old man said: " It is an easy question. Place the two snakes on a soft carpet; the one that moves about io the male, the one that keeps quiet is the female." The good man carried the answer to the king and received the reward.

Then the god asked other difficult questions which the king and his followers were unable to answer, of course, but which the good man after consulting his aged father could always solve. Here are some of the questions and their answers. " Who is the one who, being asleep, is called the awakened one, and being awake, is called the sleeping one? " The answer is this:—It is the one who is under training for enlightenment. He is awake when compared with those who are not interested in enlightenment; he is asleep when compared with those who have already attained Enlightenment.

" How can you weigh a large elephant? " " Load it on a boat and draw a line to mark how deep the boat sinks into the water. Then afterward load the same boat with stone until it sinks to the same depth and weigh the separate stones."

" What is the meaning of the saying, A cupful of

water is more than the water of an ocean?" This is the answer: "A cupful of water given in a pure and compassionate spirit to one's parent or to a sick person has eternal merit, but the water of an ocean will some day come to an end."

"A starving man, who was reduced to skin and bones, complained, is there anyone more hungry than I?" "The man in this world who is so selfish and greedy that he does not believe in the Three Treasures, Buddha, Dharma and Brotherhood, and who does not make offering to them and to his parents and teachers, his mind is not only more hungry but he will fall into the world of hungry demons where he will suffer from hunger forever."

"Here is a plank of Candana wood; which end was the bottom of the tree?" "Float the plank on water; the end that sinks a little deeper is the end nearest the root."

"Here are two horses; how can you tell that one was the mother and the other the son?" "Feed them some hay; the mother-horse will push some of the hay toward her son."

The answers to these difficult questions pleased the god and he went away. The king was also pleased and grateful, and when he found out that the answers had come from an aged parent whom his son had secreted, he withdrew the law of abandoning aged people in the mountains and ordered that they be kindly treated.

2.   Queen of Videha in India once dreamed of an elephant

that had six ivory tusks. She coveted the tusks and besought the king to get them for her. The king loved the queen and, although the task seemed an impossible one, he offered a reward to any hunter who would get the ivory from a six-tusked elephant. It happened that there was just such an elephant in the Himalaya Mountains who was training for Buddhahood. A hunter had seen it and it had saved his life in an emergency. The hunter, blinded by the great reward and forgetting the kindness the elephant had done him, returned to the mountain to kill the elephant. The hunter knowing that the elephant was seeking Buddhahood, disguised himself in the robe of a Buddhist monk and thus catching the elephant off his guard shot it with a poisoned arrow. The elephant, knowing that its end was near and knowing that the hunter had been overcome by the worldly desire for the reward, had compassion upon him and sheltered him from the fury of the other elephants. Then the elephant asked the hunter why he had done such a foolish thing. The hunter told of the reward and confessed that he coveted the six tusks. The elephant immediately broke off the tusks by hitting them against a tree and gave them to the hunter and said to him;—" By this gift I have completed my training for Buddhahood and will be reborn in the world of men. When I become Buddha, I will help you to get rid of your three poisonous arrows of greed, anger and infatuation."

3. In a thicket at the foot of the Himalaya Mountains

there once lived a parrot who had started on the path to enlightenment. One day a fire started in the thicket and the birds and animals were in frightened confusion. The parrot feeling compassion for their fright and suffering and wishing to repay the kindnesses he had received, tried to do all it could to save them. It dipped itself in a pond and flew over the fire and shook off the drops of water to extinguish the fire. This spirit of kindness and self-sacrifice was noticed by a high god who came down from the sky and the high god said to the parrot:—" You have a gallant mind, but what good do you expect to accomplish by a few drops of water against this great conflagration? " The parrot answered:—" Nothing can be accomplished by mere strength, but everything can be accomplished by the spirit of gratitude and self-sacrifice. I will try over and over again and then in the next life." The great god was impressed by the parrot's spirit and together they extinguished the fire.

4. At one time there lived in the Himalayas a bird with one body and two heads. Once one of the heads noticed the other head eating some sweet fruit and felt jealous and said to itself:—" I will eat poison fruit." So it ate poison and the bird died.

At one time the tail and the head of a snake quarrelled as to which should be the front. The tail said to the head:—" You are always taking the lead; it is not fair, you ought to let me lead sometimes." The head answered: --" It is the law of our nature that I should be the head;

I can not change places with you." But the quarrel went on and one day the tail fastened itself to a root and thus prevented the head from proceeding. When the head became tired with the struggle the tail had its own way, with the result that the snake fell into a pit of fire and perished.

In the world of nature there always exists an appropriate order and everything has its own function. If this order is disturbed, the functioning is interrupted and the organism suffers.

5. One day a couple of men were standing in front of a house discussing the man who lived there. One said to the other:—" He is a nice man but is very temperamental, he has a hot temper and gets angry quickly." The man overheard the remark, rushed out of the house and attacked the two men, striking and kicking them. If he had been a wise man he would have thanked them for their kindness, but being a foolish man he proved that they were right.

Once there was a wealthy but foolish man. He envied an other man his beautiful three-story house and made up his mind to have one just like it. He called a carpenter and ordered him to build it. The carpenter consented and immediately began the first story. The wealthy man noticed it with irritation and said:—" I don't want a foundation or a second story, I just want the beautiful third story. Build it quickly."

A foolish man always thinks of results, but is im-

patient with the effort that is necessary to get a good result.
No good result can be attained without proper effort, just
as there can be no third story without a foundation and a
first story and a second story.

A foolish man was once boiling honey. His friend
suddenly appeared and the foolish man wanted to offer
him some honey, but it was too hot, so without removing
it from the fire he fanned it to get it cool. In like manner
it is imposible to get the honey of cool wisdom without
first removing the fires of worldly passion.

6. Once there were two demons who spent a whole day
arguing and quarrelling about a box, a cane and a pair of
shoes. A man passing by, enquired, " Why are you arguing about these things? What magical properties have
they that you should be quarrelling about their possession?"

The demons explained to him that from the box they
could get anything they desired, food, clothing or treasure;
with the cane they could subdue all their enemies; and
with the pair of shoes they could travel through the air.
The man said: " Why quarrel? If you will go away for
a few minutes, I can think of a fair division of the things
between you." So the two demons retired and as soon
as they were gone, the man put on the shoes, seized the
box and the cane and was off through the air.

The " demons " represent men of different beliefs. "A
box " means the gifts that are made in charity; men do
not realise how many treasures can be produced from

charity. "The cane" means the practice of Dhyana.
Men do not realise that by the practice of spiritual concentration of mind they can subdue all worldly desires.
"A pair of shoes" means the Paramitas, the pure ideals
of thought and conduct, that will carry them beyond all
desire and all argument. Why should people argue and
quarrel about a box, a cane and a pair of shoes?

Once upon a time a man was travelling alone and
came to a vacant house and it being dusk he decided to
spend the night there. About midnight a demon brought
in a corpse and left it on the floor. Later another demon
appeared and claimed the corpse as his and they quarrelled
over it.

Then the first demon said it was useless to argue
about it further and proposed that they refer it to a judge
to decide the possession. The other demon agreed to
this and seeing the man cowering in the corner asked him
to decide the ownership. The man was badly frightened
for he well knew that whatever decision he made would
anger the demon that lost and that the losing demon would
seek revenge, but he decided to tell truthfully just what he
had witnessed. As he expected, this angered the second
demon who grabbed one of the man's arms and tore it
off, but the first demon replaced the arm by one taken
from the corpse. The angry demon tore away the man's
other arm, but the first demon immediately replaced that
by the other arm of the corpse. And so it went on until
both arms, both legs, the head and the body had been
successively torn away and replaced by the corresponding

parts of the corpse. Then the two demons, seeing the parts of the man scattered about on the floor, picked them up and devoured them and went away chuckling.

The poor man who had taken refuge in the deserted house was very much upset by his misfortunes. The parts of his body which the demons had eaten were the parts his parents had given him, and the parts that he now had belonged to the corpse. Who was he, anyway? Realising all the facts he was unable to figure it out and, becoming crazy, he wandered out into the town. Coming to a temple, he went in and told his troubles to the monks. They told him that if he could understand the problem of "egolessness," he would be all right again. But what is egolessness?

7. Once a beautiful and well dressed woman visited a house. The master of the house asked her who she was; she replied that she was the goddess of wealth. The master of the house was delighted and treated her nicely. Soon after another woman appeared who was ugly looking and poorly dressed. The master asked who she was and the woman replied that she was goddess of poverty. The master was frightened and tried to get her out of the house, but woman refused to depart, saying. "The gooddess of wealth is my sister. There is an agreement between us that we are never to live separately; if you chase me out, she goes with me." But the master was so afraid of her that he put her out and when he returned the other woman had disappeared also.

Birth goes with death. Fortune goes with misfortune. Bad things follow good things. Foolish people dread misfortune and strive after good fortune, but wise men ignore differences of fortune and thus are not disturbed by their passing.

8. Once there lived a poor artist who left his home to seek his fortune. After three years of hard struggle he had saved three hundred pieces of gold and decided to return to his home. On his way he came to a great temple in which a grand ceremony was in progress. He was greatly impressed by it and thought to himself:—" Hitherto I have thought only of the present; I have never considered my future happiness. It is a part of my good fortune that I have come to this good place; I must take advantage of it to plant seeds of merit." Thinking thus he gratefully donated all his savings to the temple and returned to his home penniless. When he reached his home, his wife reproached him for not bringing her some money for her support. The poor artist replied that he had saved some money but had put it where it would be safe. When she pressed him to tell her where he had hidden it, he confessed that he had given it to the monks at a certain temple. This made the wife angry and she scolded her husband and finally carried the matter to the local judge. When the judge asked the artist for his defence, the artist said that he had not acted foolishly, for he had saved the money after a long and hard struggle and wanted to use it as seed for future good fortune. When he came to the

temple it seemed to him that there was the field where he should plant his gold as seed for good fortune. Then he added:—"As I gave the monks the gold, I seemed to be throwing away all greed and stinginess, and seemed to be gaining true wisdom." The judge praised the artist's spirit, and those who were present manifested their approval by helping him to find good employment. Thus the artist and his wife entered into permanent good fortune.

9. A man living near to a cemetery heard one night a voice calling to him from a grave. He was too timid to investigate it himself but the next day he told it to a braver friend. This friend went to the cemetery the following night and, sure enough, the voice was heard issuing from a grave. The friend asked who it was and what it wanted. The voice replied:—"I am a hidden treasure that has decided to give itself to someone. I offered it to a man last night but he was too timid to come after it, so I will give it to you. Tomorrow morning I will come to your house with my seven followers."

The friend said:—"I will be waiting for you, but please tell me how I am to treat you?" The voice replied:—"We will come in monk's robes. Have a room ready for us with hot water to wash our feet and hands, and seats for us and eight bowls of gruel. After the meal, you are to lead us one by one into a closed room when we will transform ourselves into crocks of gold."

The next morning the friend prepared the room just

as he was told and waited for the monks to appear. In due time they appeared and the friend received them courteously and after they had eaten the food he led them into the closed room, when each monk turned himself into a crock of gold.

There was a very envious and greedy man in the same village who learned of the incident and he invited eight monks to his house. After their meal he led them into a closed room, but not turning themselves into crocks of gold, he became angry and treated them roughly and the police came and punished the man.

As for the timid man, when he heard that the voice from the grave had brought wealth to the brave man, he went to the house of the brave man and demanded the gold, saying that it was his, because the voice was first addressed to him. The brave man said he could have the crocks, but when the timid man opened them he found them containing snakes that attacked him.

The king heard about the matter and ruled that the crocks belonged to the brave man and uttered the following observation:—" Everything in the world goes like this. Foolish people are avaricious for good results but are too timid to go after them and, therefore, are continually failing. These foolish and timid people think only of external things, they do not have either faith or courage to face the internal things of mind by which alone true success is attained."

CHAPTER TWO

THE WAY OF PRACTICAL ATTAINMENT

I

SEARCH FOR TRUTH

1. In the search for truth there are certain questions that are immaterial. Of what material is the universe constructed? Is the universe eternal? Are there limits to the universe? What is the ideal form of organization of human society? These questions have no vital relation to enlightenment. If one were to postpone the search and practice for enlightenment until such questions were cleared, he would die before he found the Path.

Suppose a man was pierced by a poisoned arrow, and a surgeon was called to extract the arrow, but the man objected, saying, " Wait a little. Before you begin, I want to know who shot this arrow? Was it a man or a woman? Was it some one of noble birth, or was it peasant? Was it a big bow, or a small bow, that shot the arrow? What was the bow-string made of? Was it made of fiber, or of gut? Was the arrow made of rattan, or of reed? What feathers were used? Before you extract the arrow, I want to know all about these things." Before all this information can be secured, the poison will have time to circulate all through the system; the man may die before it is secured. The first duty is to remove the arrow with its poison.

When a fire of passion is endangering the world, the composition of the universe matters little. The question of whether the universe has limits or is eternal can wait until some way is found to extinguish the fires; and so can the question as to whether the present organization of society is ideal or not. In the face of the problems of birth, old age, sickness and death; in the presence of lamentation, sorrow, suffering and pain; one should first search for a way to end them and then devote himself to the practice of that way.

The Buddha's Dharma teaches what it is important to know and not what is unimportant. That is, it teaches people that they must learn what they should learn, remove what they should remove, train for what they should train, become enlightened about what they should become enlightened. Therefore, people should first discern what is of first importance, what problem should first be solved, what is the first misfortune to be expected. To do all this, they must first undertake the training of the mind, that is, they must first seek mind-control.

2. Suppose a man goes to the forest to get some of the pith that grows in the center of a tree and returns with a burden of branches and leaves thinking that he has secured what he went after; would he not be foolish? But that is what many people are doing. A person seeks a path that will lead him away from birth, old age, sick-

ness and death, or from lamentation, sorrow, suffering and pain, then he follows the path a little way and notices some little advance and immediately he becomes proud and conceited and domineering. He is like the man who sought pith and went away satisfied with a burden of leaves. Another man becoming satisfied with the progress he has made by a little effort, relaxes his effort and becomes proud and conceited, he is carrying away only a load of branches.

Still another man finding that his mind is becoming calmer and his thoughts clearer, he too relaxes his effort and becomes proud and conceited; he has a burden of the bark of the tree. Then again, another man becomes proud and conceited because he notices that he has gained a measure of intuitive insight; he has a load of the woody fiber of the tree. All of these seekers who become easily satisfied by their effort and become proud and over-bearing relax their effort and easily fall into idleness. Such people will inevitably again face suffering.

Those who seek the true path to enlightenment must not expect an easy task nor one made pleasant by offers of respect and honor and devotion. And more, they must not aim at a little slight effort, or a trifling advance in calmness or knowledge or insight. They must aim at the high and difficult goal of perfection;—perfect insight, perfect enlightenment, perfect calmness. There is no place for relaxation of effort or self praise until Buddhahood is attained.

3. First of all, one should get clearly in mind the basic and essential nature of this world of life and death. It has no self-substance of its own. It is simply a vast concordance of causes and conditions that have had their origin solely and exclusively, in the activities of the mind as it has been stimulated by ignorance, false imaginations, desires and infatuation. It is not something external about which the mind has false conceptions; it has no substance whatever. It has come into appearance by the processes of the mind itself, manifesting its own delusions. It is founded and built-up out of the desires of the mind, out of its sufferings and struggle incident to the pain caused by its own greed, anger and infatuation. Its ultimate source is ignorance, it is shrouded in the darkness of delusion, it appears through suffering and sorrow. There is nothing but mind and when it is uncontrolled it fashions a fanciful and everchanging dream-world of delusion. Those who aim at enlightenment should get this clearly in mind, and then proceed to fight it out with mind through mind.

4. Oh my mind! Why do you hover so restlessly over the changing circumstances of life? Why do you make me so confused and restless? Why do you urge me to collect so many things? You are like a plow that you break in pieces just as you begin to plow; you are like a rudder that you dismantle just as you are venturing out on the sea of life and death. Of what use are many rebirths if we make no good use of this life?

Oh my mind! Once you caused me to be born as a king, and then you caused me to be born as an outcast and to beg my food. Sometimes you cause me to be born in heavenly mansions of the gods and to dwell in luxury and in ecstasy, then you plunge me into the flames of hell.

Oh my foolish, foolish mind! Thus you have led me along different paths and I have been obedient to you and docile. But now that I have heard Buddha's Dharma, do not disturb me any more nor cause me further sufferings, but together, humbly and patiently, let us seek enlightenment.

Oh my mind! If you could only learn that everything is empty and transitory; if you could only learn not to grasp after things, not to covet things, not to give way to greed, anger and foolishness; then we might journey in quietness. Then, by severing the bonds of desire by the sword of wisdom, being undisturbed by changing circumstances good or bad, loss or gain, we might dwell in peace.

Oh my dear mind! It was you who first awakened faith, it was you who suggested our seeking enlightenment. Why do you give way so easily to greed, love of comfort and pleasant excitement?

Oh my mind! Why do you rush hither and thither with no definite purpose? Let us cross this wild sea of delusion. Hitherto I have acted as you wished, but now you must act as I wish and, together, we will follow the Buddha's Dharma.

Oh my dear mind! These mountains, rivers and seas are changeable and pain-producing. Where in this world of delusion shall we seek quietness? Let us follow the Buddha's Dharma and cross over to the other shore of Enlightenment.

5. Those who really seek the path to enlightenment must dictate terms to the mind. Then they must proceed with strong determination. Even though they are abused by some and scorned by others they must go forward with undisturbed mind. They must not become angry though they are beaten by fists, or hit by stones, or gashed by swords. Even if enemies saw off the head from the body, the mind must not be disturbed. If they let their mind become darkened by the things they suffer, they are not following the teaching of Buddha. On the contrary they must take advantage of their enemie's treatment to return kindness for injury. They must determine, no matter what happens to them, to remain steadfast, unmovable, ever radiating thoughts of compassion and good-will. Let abuse come, let misfortune come, one should resolve to remain unmoved and tranquil in mind.

For the sake of enlightenment, I will accomplish the impossible, I will endure the unendurable. I will give to the uttermost. If I am told that to gain enlightenment I must limit my food to a single grain of rice a day, I will eat only one grain of rice. If the path of enlightenment leads through fire, I will go forward through fire.

But one must not do these things for any ulterior purpose. One should do them because it is the wise thing, the right thing, to do. One should do them out of a spirit of compassion, as a mother does things for her little child, for her sick child, with no thought of her own strength or comfort.

6. Once there was a king who loved his people and his country and ruled them with wisdom and kindness and, because of it, his country was prosperous and peaceful. He was always seeking for greater wisdom and enlightenment; he even offered rewards to anyone who could lead him to worthy teachers.

His worth and wisdom finally came to the attention of the gods, but they determined to test him. A god disguised as a demon appeared before the gates of the king's palace and asked to be brought before the king as he had a holy teaching for him. The king sent for him and asked for instruction. The demon took on a dreadful form and demanded food, saying that he could not teach until he had the food he liked. Choice food was offered the demon, but he insisted that he must have the warm flesh and blood of a human. The crown-prince offered his body and the queen offered her body, but still the demon was unsatisfied and demanded the body of the king. The king expressed his willingness to give his body, but asked that he might first hear the teaching so that he could benefit his country by it.

Suddenly the god uttered the following wise teaching: —" Lamentation rises from desire and fear rises from desire. Those who remove desire have no lamentation and no fear." Suddenly the god resumed the true form and the prince and the queen also appeared among them.

7. Once there was a seeker of the true path who visited the Himalayas in search of good teaching. He cared nothing for all the treasures of earth or for all the delights of heaven, but he sought the teaching that would remove all mental delusions.

The gods were impressed by the man's earnestness and sincerity and decided to test his sincerity. So one of the gods manifested himself as a demon and appeared in the Himalayas singing: "Everything changes, everything appears and disappears." The seeker heard this song and it pleased him very much. It pleased him as though, being thirsty, he had found a spring of cool water, or as though, being in bondage, he had suddenly been set free. He said to himself, at last I have found the true teaching that I have sought for so long.

He followed the voice and at last came upon the frightful demon. With uneasy mind he approached the demon and said:—"Was it you who sang the holy song that I have just heard? If it was you, please sing more of it."

The demon replied:—"Yes, it was my song, but I can not sing more of it until I have had something to eat, I am starving."

The good man begged him very earnestly to sing more of it, saying:—"It has a sacred meaning to me and I have sought its teaching for a long time. I have only heard a part of it, please let me hear more of it."

The demon said again, and this time more threateningly:—"I am starving, but if I can taste warm flesh and the blood of a man, I will finish the song."

The good man in his eagerness to hear the teaching promised the demon that he could have his body after he had heard the teaching. Then the demon sang the complete song:—

> Everything changes,
> Everything appears and disappears;
> There is no blissful peace
> Until one passes beyond both life and extinction.

Hearing this, the good man quietly climbed a tree and hurled himself down at the feet of the demon, but the demon had disappeared and a radiant god received the body of the good man unharmed.

8. Once upon a time there was an earnest seeker of the path that leads to enlightenment, named Sadaprarudita. He cast aside every temptation to profit and honor and sought it at the risk of his life. One day a voice from heaven came to him, saying:—"Go straight toward the east. Do not think of either heat or cold, pay no attention to worldly praise or scorn, do not be bothered by questions of good or evil, but just keep on going east. In the far east you will find a true teacher and will gain enlightenment."

Sadaprarudita was very pleased to get this definite

instruction and immediately started on his journey eastward. Sometimes there was no path going in the direction but he pressed on sleeping where night found him
in a lonely field or in the wild mountains. Being a
stranger in a strange land he suffered many humiliations;
once he sold himself into slavery, selling his own flesh
from hunger, but at last he found the true teacher.

There is a saying. " Good things are costly," and
Sadaprarudita found it true in his case, for even after he
had found the true teacher he had many difficulties in
reaching his presence. He had no flowers to offer the
teacher and no money with which to reward him. He
tried to sell his services but could find no one to hire him.
There seemed to be an evil spirit hindering him every way
he turned. The path to enlightenment is a hard one, it
may cost a man his life. At last Sadaprarudita reached
the presence of the teacher and then he had a new difficulty, he had no paper on which to take notes of the
master's teaching, and no brush and no ink. Then he
punctured his wrist and took notes in his own blood.
In this way he secured the precious truth.

9. Once there was a boy named Sudhana who wished for
enlightenment and who earnestly sought the way. He
went to many different teachers. From a fisherman he
learned the lore of the sea and it suggested the tempests
and waves on the great ocean of life and death. From a
doctor he learned compassion toward sick people in their
suffering. From a wealthy man he learned that saving

pennies was the secret of his fortune and he thought how necessary it is to conserve every trifling gain on the path to enlightenment. From a meditating monk he learned that the pure and peaceful mind had a miraculous power to purify and tranquillize other minds. Once he met a woman of exceptional personality and was impressed by her benevolent spirit and from her he learned a lesson that charity was the fruit of wisdom. Once he met an aged wanderer who told him that to reach a certain place he had to scale a mountain of swords and pass through a valley of fire. From him he learned that he must be dauntless on his own journey to enlightenment. Thus Sudhana learned from his experiences that there was true teaching to be gained from everything one sees or hears.

But besides learning from people's words and teaching, Sudhana received instruction from many other sources. He learned patience from a poor, physically imperfect woman; he learned a lesson of simple happiness from watching children playing in the street; from some gentle and humble people, who never thought of wanting anything that anybody else wanted, he learned the secret of living at peace with all the world.

He learned a lesson of harmony from watching the blending of the elements of incense, and a lesson of thanks-giving from the offerings of flowers. One day in passing through a forest he rested under a noble tree and noticed near by a tiny seedling growing out of a fallen and decayed tree and it taught him a lesson of impermanence.

One day in making his way over the high mountains and taking advantage of the contour of the peaks and valleys to make his path as easy as possible, he thought to himself, " In this same manner I must take advantage of the varied experiences of life to find a path for the mind in its search for enlightenment.   His mind often became arid and parched from the flaming wish of his heart for enlightenment, but the friendly sunlight by day and the twinkling stars by night constantly refreshed his spirit. Thus Sudhana profited by the experiences of his long journey.

Indeed, those who seek for enlightenment must think of their minds as castles that must be built strong and resistant without but convenient and beautiful within. They must close the castle gates against enemies, but they must open them wide for Buddha and respectfully and humbly invite him to enter the inmost fastness, there to offer him the fragrant incense of faith and the flowers of gratitude and gladness.

II

THE WAY OF PRACTICE

1. For those who are seeking enlightenment, there are three methods of practice that must be understood and followed. First, rules for practical behavior; second, right concentration of mind; and third, wisdom.

Every man, whether he be a common man or an ascetic, should follow the precepts for good behavior. He should control both his mind and body, he should guard the gates of his five senses.   He should be afraid of even a trifling forgetfulness and from moment to moment should endeavor to practise only good deeds.

What is meant by concentration of mind? It means, not becoming attached to thoughts and desires as they arise, not permitting new thoughts to arise, and then to hold the mind pure and tranquil.

What is wisdom? It is wisdom to perfectly understand and to patiently accept the Four Noble Truths; to know the fact of suffering and its nature; to know the source of suffering; to know what constitutes the end of suffering; to know the Noble Path that leads to the end of suffering. Those who are earnestly following these three methods of practice may rightly be called disciples of Buddha.

Supposing a donkey was following a herd of cows and loudly proclaiming, " Look, I am a cow." Would any one believe him? It is just as foolish for a man who does not follow the three methods of practice, to boast that he is a disciple of Buddha.

Before a farmer gathers a harvest he must first plow the ground, sow the seed, irrigate, and remove the weeds as they spring up in springtime. Just so the seeker for enlightenment must follow the three methods of practice. A farmer does not expect to see buds today, to see plants tomorrow, to gather a harvest the day after. Neither can one who seeks enlightenment expect to remove worldly desires to-day, to remove attachments and habits tomorrow, and to get enlightenment the day after. Just as plants receive the patient care of the farmer after the seed has been sown and during the changes of climate and during the growth from plant to seed, so the seeker for enlightenment must patiently and perseveringly cultivate the soil of enlightenment by following the three methods of practice. If he does this he will surely see the weeds of worldly desires gradually disappear, he will see the plant of right knowledge growing steadily, and in due time he will receive the harvest of enlightenment.

2. It is difficult to advance along the path that leads to enlightenment so long as one is covetous of comforts and luxuries and letting his mind be disturbed by the desires of the senses. There is a wide difference between the enjoyment of life and the enjoyment of the Dharma.

As has been explained, mind is the source of all things. If the mind enjoys worldly affairs, illusions and suffering will inevitably follow, but if the mind enjoys the Dharma, happiness, contentment and enlightenment will just as surely follow. Therefore, those who are seeking enlightenment should keep their minds pure and patiently practise the three methods. If they keep the precepts it will be natural to practise concentration of mind, and if they practice concentration it will be just as natural for them to practise wisdom, and wisdom will lead them to enlightenment.

Indeed, these three methods (keeping the precepts, practising concentration of mind and always acting wisely) are the true path to enlightenment. If people do not follow these three methods, they accumulate mental delusions. They can only get enlightenment by following this true path. They must not argue with worldly people about it, but they must patiently meditate in this inner world of a pure mind.

3. If the three methods of practice are analysed they reveal the Eightfold Noble Path, (namely, Right Observation, Right Thought, Right Speech, Right Behavior, Right Livelihood, Right Effort, Right Mindfulness, Right Concentration), the four points to be considered, the four right procedures, the five faculties to be employed, and the six paths of right effort.

Right Observation means to thoroughly understand the Four Noble Truths, to observe things truly and not to be deceived by appearances and desires. Right Thought means the resolution not to cherish desires, not to be fearful nor angry, not to harm any living thing. Right Speech means the avoidance of lying words, idle words, abusive words, double-tongued. Right Behavior means the practice of kindness, the practice of honesty, the practice of purity. Right Livelihood means to avoid any life that would bring shame to a man. Right Effort means to be guided by right spiritual ideals. Right Mindfulness means to maintain a pure and thoughtful mind. Right Concentration means to keep the mind pure and tranquil seeking to realise the mind's pure essence.

There are four points to be considered:—First, to consider the body impure, to seek to remove all attachments to it. Second, to consider the senses as a source of suffering, whatever their feelings of pain or pleasure may be. Third, to consider the mind to be in a constant state of flux. Fourth, to consider everything in the world as being a concordance of causes and conditions and that nothing remains unchanged for ever.

There are four right procedures:—First, to prevent evil from starting. Second, to remove all evil as soon as it starts. Third, to induce the doing of good deeds. Fourth, to encourage the growth and continuance of good deeds that have already started. And Five Faculties of Powers;—First, faith to believe; second, the will to make the endeavor; third, the faculty of reliable memory; fourth, the ability to concentrate attention; fifth, the ability to maintain clear wisdom in the conservation of results.

4. There are Six Paths for reaching the other shore of Enlightenment;—The Path of Charity, the Path of Right Behavior, the Path of Endurance, the Path of Endeavor, the Path of Concentration of Mind, and the Path of Wisdom. By following these methods or paths one can surely pass over from the shore of Delusion to the shore of Enlightenment.

The practice of Charity gets rid of selfishness; the practice of Good Behavior keeps one thoughtful of the rights and comforts of others; the practice of Endurance helps one to control a fearful or angry mind; the practice of Endeavor helps one to be diligent and faithful; the practice of Concentration helps one to control a wandering and futile mind; the practice of Wisdom changes a dark and confused mind into a clear and penetrating insight. Charity and Good Behavior are like the foundation of a great castle. Endurance and Faith are the walls of the castle that protect against outside enemies. Concentration and Wisdom are the personal armour that protects one against the assaults of life and death.

5. If one gives a gift only after he has been importuned, or because it is easier to give than not to give, it is charity of course but it is not true Charity. True Charity gives freely from a sympathetic heart before any request has been made, and true Charity is not occasional but is constant. Neither is it true Charity if after the act there are feelings of regret or self-praise; true Charity gives with pleasure, forgetting himself as the giver, the one who has received the gift and the gift itself. True Charity springs spontaneously from a merciful heart with no thought of any return or of any inconvenience or even of life itself, desiring only that others with the self may enter into a life of Enlightenment.

6. Once there was a prince named Satta who went into the forest with his two older brothers. At the foot of a cliff they saw a famishing tigress with newly born cubs and the tigress was evidently tempted to devour them. The two elder brothers ran away in fear but Satta threw himself over the cliff in front of the tigress to save the lives of the little cubs. Prince Satta did this charitable

act spontaneously but within his mind he was thinking:—
" This body is changing and impermanent; I have loved
this body with no thought of throwing it away but now
I make it an offering that both this tigress and myself may
gain enlightenment."   This thought in the mind of Prince
Satta shows the true determination to gain enlightenment.

7.   There are Four Emotional States that the seeker for
Enlightenment should cherish;—They are mercy, tenderness, gladness and equality.   One can remove greed by
cherishing mercy; one can remove anger by tenderness;
one can remove suffering by gladness; one can remove
the habit of discrimination of enemies and friends by
cherishing an equitable mind.   It is a great mercy to remove everything that does not tend to make people happy
and contented; it is a great tenderness to make people
happy and contented; it is a great gladness to see everyone happy and contented; there is great peacefulness
when everyone is happy and contented, then one can have
equal feelings toward everybody.

With care one may cherish these four emotional states
and develop them until they are habitual, but it is not an
easy thing to do.   An evil mind is as hard to get rid of
as a watch dog, and a right mind is as easy to lose as a
deer in a forest; or an evil mind is as hard to remove as
letters carved in stone, and a right mind is as easy to lose
as words written in water.   Indeed, it is the most difficult
thing in life to train oneself for enlightenment.

8.   There was a disciple of the Blessed One whose name was Srona.   He was born in a wealthy family and was a young man of delicate health, but he was very earnest to gain enlightenment and, it is said, that he tried so hard that his feet sweat blood.   The Blessed One pitied him and said to him;—" Srona, my boy, did you ever study playing the harp in your home?   You know that a harp does not make music if the strings are stretched too much or too little.   It only makes music when the strings are stretched just right.

" The training for enlightenment is just like tuning a harp.   One can not attain enlightenment if he is idle, but neither can he attain enlightenment if he stretches the strings of his mind too tightly.   One must be considerate and act wisely."   Srona profited by these words and finally gained what he sought.

9.   Once there was a prince, who was skilful in the use of the five weapons.   One day he was returning to his home from his practice and met a monster whose skin was invulnerable.   The monster started for him but nothing daunted.   The prince shot an arrow at him which fell harmless.   Then he threw his spear which failed to penetrate the thick skin.   Then he threw the bar and the javelin but they made no impression.   Then he drew his sword but the sword broke.   Then the prince attacked the monster with his hands and feet but to no purpose for the monster clutched him in his giant arms and held him fast.   Then the prince tried to use his head but in vain.

The monster said;—" It is useless for you to resist, I am going to devour you." But the prince answered;— " You may think that I am helpless, but I still have one weapon left. If you devour me, I will destroy you from your stomach." The courage of the prince disturbed the monster and he asked. " How can you do that?" The prince replied:—" By the power of the Truth." Then the monster released him and begged for instruction in the Truth.

The teaching of this fable is to encourage disciples to be persevering in their efforts and to be undaunted in the face of many reverses.

10. Both offensive self-assertion and shamelessness offend mankind, but dishonor and shame protect mankind. People respect their parents and elders, they respect their older brothers and sisters, because they are sensitive to dishonor and shame. After self-reflection it is meritorious to withhold honor from the self and to feel ashamed by observing other people.

If a man possesses a repentant spirit his sins will disappear, but if he has an unrepentant spirit his sins will continue and he must be condemned. A man who merely hears the Dharma with his ears, has not received it; it is only the one who hears it rightly and who considers its meaning and its relation to himself that can receive it and profit by it. If a man loves worldly affairs, enjoys idle talk, falls asleep while he is in training, he will fail in his search for enlightenment.

Faith, humility, shame, sincerity of effort and wisdom are the great sources of strength to him who is seeking enlightenment; among them wisdom is the greatest and all the rest are but aspects of wisdom.

11. In training for enlightenment, some may succeed quickly and others more slowly; therefore, one should not be troubled to see others becoming enlightened. When a man is practising archery he does not expect an early success but he knows that if he practises patiently that he will become more and more accurate. A river begins as a little brook but grows ever larger until it flows into the great ocean. Like these examples, if one trains with patience and perseverence, he will surely gain enlightenment.

As it has been explained, if one keeps his eyes open, he will see the teaching everywhere, so his opportunities for advancement are endless. Once there was a man who was offering incense at an altar and he noticed that the fragrance was neither coming nor going, it neither appeared nor disappeared; from this mere trifle, he suddenly gained enlightenment. Once there was a man who got a thorn into his foot. He felt the sharp pain and the thought came to him, that pain was only a reaction of the mind. From that chance a deeper thought followed, a mind may get out of hand if one fails to control it, or it may become pure if one succeeds. From these thoughts a little later, enlightenment came to him.

There was another man who was very avaricious.

One day he was thinking of his greedy mind when the thought came to him, greedy thoughts are but shavings and kindlings that wisdom can kindle and consume. That thought was the beginning of his enlightenment.

There is an old saying:—" Keep your mind level. If the mind is level, the whole world will be level." Consider these words. Realise that all the distinctions of the world are but observations of a mind. There is a path to enlightenment in those very words. Indeed, the ways to Enlightenment are endless.

III
THE WAY OF FAITH

1. Those who take refuge in the three treasures, Buddha, Dharma and Brotherhood, are called disciples of Buddha. The disciples of Buddha observe four norms of mind-control, namely, the precepts, faith, charity and wisdom. The disciples of Buddha practise the five precepts;—not to kill any living creature, not to steal, not to act impurely, not to lie, and not to use intoxicants of any kind. The disciples of Buddha have faith in Buddha's perfect wisdom. The disciples of Buddha try to keep away from greediness and selfishness and to practise charity. The disciples of Buddha, understanding the law of co-operating causes and keeping in mind the transiency of life, conform to the norm of wisdom.

A tree leaning toward the east will fall eastward and those who listen to the Buddha's Dharma and maintain faith in it will be reborn in the Buddha's Pure Land.

2.   It has just been said that those who believe in the
three treasures, Buddha, Dharma and the Brotherhood,
are called, the disciples of Buddha.   Buddha is the one
who attained perfect Enlightenment and used his attainment to emancipate and bless all mankind.   The Dharma
is the truth and the spirit of Enlightenment and the teachings that explain it.   The Brotherhood is the perfect
fellowship of believers in Buddha and the Dharma.   It
has no limits of space nor time but radiates always and
everywhere the spirit of Buddha and the truth of the
Dharma.   The Brotherhood is the happy gathering of
those who are radiating the spirit of Buddha and teaching
the Dharma and of those who are awakening faith in
Buddha and the Dharma.

We speak of Buddhahood, Dharma and Brotherhood
as though they were three different things, but they are
really only one.   Buddha is manifested in his Dharma and
is realised by the Brotherhood.   Therefore, to believe in
the Dharma and to cherish the Brotherhood is to have
faith in Buddha, and to have faith in Buddha means to
believe in the Dharma and to cherish the Brotherhood.
Therefore, people are emancipated and enlightened simply
by having faith in Buddha.   Buddha is the perfectly Enlightened One and he loves everybody as though each was
his only son.   So if anyone regards Buddha as his own
parent, he identifies himself with Buddha and attains
enlightenment.   Those who thus regard Buddha will be

supported by his wisdom and perfumed by his grace.

3. Nothing in the world brings greater benefit than to believe in Buddha.   Just hearing Buddha's name, believing and being pleased by it for a moment is rewarding. Therefore one must please himself seeking the teaching even through the conflagration that is over all the world. It will be hard to meet a teacher who can explain the Dharma, it will be harder to meet a Buddha, but it will be hardest to become a worthy disciple.

But now that you have met the Dharma that is hard to meet, and have had it explained to you that is hard to understand, you ought to rejoice and believe and have faith in Buddha.

4. On the long journey of human life, faith is the best of companions, faith is the best refreshment by the way, and the greatest reward at the end.   Faith is the hand that receives the Dharma, faith is the hand that receives the profit.   Faith removes greed, fear and pride; faith teaches courtesy and wins respect, faith frees one from the bondage of circumstances, faith gives one courage to meet hardship, faith gives one power to overcome temptation, faith enables one to keep his deeds bright and pure, faith enriches the mind with wisdom.   Faith is the fire that consumes all the impurities of worldly desire, faith removes the burden, faith is the guide that leads the way, faith is the encouragement when the way is long and wearisome, faith brings one to enlightenment.

Faith brings us in the presence of Buddha, faith brings us to where Buddha's arm supports us.   Faith softens the hard and selfish minds of people and gives them a friendly spirit and a mind of understanding sympathy.

5.   Those who have faith have the wisdom to recognise Buddha's teaching in whatever they hear.   Those who have faith have the wisdom to see that everything is but the appearance that arises from co-operating causes and conditions, and then faith gives them the grace of patient acceptance and the ability to conform to conditions peacefully.   Faith gives them the wisdom to recognise the transiency of life and the grace not to be surprised or grieved at whatever comes or with the passing of life itself, knowing that however conditions and appearances may change, the trueness of life remains unchanged.

Faith has three significant aspects:—a humble and patient self-depreciation, a rejoicing and sincere respect for the virtues of others, and a grateful acceptance of Buddha's appearance.   Every one should cultivate these aspects of faith; they should be sensitive to their failings and their impurities, they should be ashamed of them and confess them; they should diligently practise the recognition of the good traits and good deeds of others and praise them for them, they should habitually desire to act with Buddha and to love with Buddha.

The mind of faith is the mind of sincerity; it is a deep mind, an unquestioning mind, a mind that is sincerely glad to be led to Buddha's Pure Land by Buddha's power

and in his own way. Therefore, Buddha gives a power
to faith that leads people to the Pure Land, a power that
purifies them, a power that protects them from self-delus-
ion. Even if they have faith only for a moment, when
they hear the Buddha's name, that is praised all over the
world, it will bring them to his Pure Land.

6. Faith is not something that is added to the worldly
mind—it is the mind's true nature of Buddhahood. In
most minds Buddha-nature is defiled and deeply covered
by ignorance and worldly passion, but faith uncovers the
true Buddha-nature and discovers it, because one who
understands Buddha is Buddha himself; one who has
faith in Buddha is Buddha himself.

But it is difficult to uncover and recover one's true
nature; it is difficult to maintain a pure mind in the constant rise and fall of greed, anger and worldly passion,
but faith enables one to do it.

Within the forest of Eranda there is said to grow
the poisonous Eranda tree that grows nowhere else, and
that the sweet Candana tree will not grow there.

It is a miracle if a Candana tree grows in an Eranda
forest. It is a like miracle if faith in Buddha grows in
the heart of worldly people. Therefore, the faith to believe in Buddha is called a " rootless " faith. That is, it
has no root by which it can grow in the human mind, but
it has a root to grow in the merciful mind of Buddha.
Thus faith is fruitful and sacred.

7. But faith is hard to awaken in an easy-going mind. In the path to enlightenment the difficulties are very great and one can not easily overcome them. In particular there are five suspicions that lurk in the shadows of the human mind and which tend to discourage faith. First, there is doubt of the Buddha's wisdom; second, there is doubt in the Buddha's teaching; third, there is doubt of the personality that is explaining Buddha's teachings; fourth, there is doubt as to whether the ways and methods suggested for following the Noble Path are reliable; and fifth, there is doubt as to whether others who are seeking to understand the Dharma and follow Buddha's teachings are sincere, which tends to make one arrogant and impatient.

Indeed, there is nothing more dreadful than the habit of doubt. Faith draws people together, but doubt separates them. It is a poison that disintegrates friendships and breaks up pleasant relations. It is a thorn that irritates and hurts; it is a sword that kills. One should beware of cherishing a mind of doubt.

8. The beginnings of faith were planted by the compassion of Buddha, long ago. When one has faith he should realise this fact and be very grateful to Buddha for his goodness. They should never forget that it is not because of their own merit that they have awakened faith, but because it was Buddha's merit which long ago threw its pure light of faith into human minds and dispelled the darkness of their ignorance, and you who have present faith have entered into their heritage.

In spite of living an ordinary life, one can be born in the Pure Land, as we awaken faith through Buddha's long continued mercy.

It is, indeed, hard to be born in this world, but it is harder to be reborn in Buddha's Pure Land. It is hard to hear the Dharma, it is harder to awaken faith; therefore every one should try his best to hear the Dharma, and respond to Buddha's love.

IV

THE WAY OF CONCENTRATION

1. If a disciple is to be successful in the practice of concentration, he must observe four things. First. He must have a clear understanding that all things are only manifestations of the mind itself. Second. He must discard the notion of birth, abiding and disappearance. Third. He must clearly understand the egolessness of both things and persons. And fourth. He must have a true conception of what constitutes self-realization of Noble Wisdom. He must understand that it is based upon identity and oneness and emptiness, and there is nothing to be discriminated or predicated concerning it.

When a disciple is no longer attached to words and their meanings, he will be able to establish himself where there will be "a turning about" in the deepest seat of consciousness by means of which he will be able to attain self-realization of Noble Wisdom.

2.   There are two aspects of self-realization, namely, the teachings about it and the realization itself. The teachings as varioulsy given in the Doctrinal works are intended to awaken in all beings a true perception of the Dharma.   They are designed to keep one away from all dualistic notions of being and non being, of oneness and otherness.

Realization itself is within the inner consciousness. It is an inner experience that has no connection with the lower mind system and its discriminations of words, ideas and philosophical speculations.   It shines out with its own clear light to reveal the error and foolishness of mind-constructed teachings, to render impotent all evil influences from without, and to guide one unerringly to the realm of truth.

3.   There are four kinds of Dhyana practice. First. The Dhyana practised by the ignorant who do now understand its purpose and with whom it becomes sitting still with vacant minds.   This is also the Dhyana practised by those who, seeing the body as a shadow and skeleton full of suffering and impurity, despise it and seek to attain emancipation from it by the mere cessation of thought. Second.   The Dhyana devoted to the examination of meaning is practised by those who, perceiving the untenability of such ideas as self, other and both, and who have passed beyond the twofold egolessness, devote Dhyana to an examination of the significance of egolessness and

the fifferentiations of the Bodhisattva stages. Third.
The Dhyana with essence, or oneness, or the Divine
name for its object, is practised by those earnest disciples
and masters who, while fully recognising the twofold
egolessness and the imagelessness of Essence, yet cling
to the notion of an ultimate suchness. Fourth. The
Dhyana of Buddhas is practised by those who have entered
upon the stage of Buddhahood and who, abiding in the
triple bliss which characterises the self-realization of
Noble Wisdom, are devoting themselves for the sake of
all beings to the accomplishment of incomprehensible
words for their emancipation. This is the pure Dhyana
of the Buddha where all lesser things and ideas are trans-
cended and forgotten and there remains only a perfect
state of imagelessness.

4. Those who practise Dhyana should retire to solitary
place and, sitting erect, should definitely seek to tranquillize the mind. Do not fix the thoughts on the breath,
do not let the thoughts dwell on what you have seen,
heard, learned or memorised. All particularisations and
discriminations, all recollections and imaginations should
be excluded from conscious thought, and even the idea
of exclusion should be excluded, because, the mind if
it is to be tranquillized, must be like mind essence, that is,
be devoid of all attributes, free of all distinctions, calm
and undisturbed.

There are two aspects of Dhyana, first there is the
effort to suppress idle thinking, and second, there is an

effort of concentration to realize this emptiness and purity. At first a beginner will have to practise these separately, but as he gains in mind-control, the two efforts will merge into one.

In conscious thinking, thoughts are preceeded by perception, perception by sensation, and sensation by some external stimulus, so one who is seeking to tranquillize his mind should first abandon the notion of an external world and should concentrate attention on the empty aspect of mind-essence. That is, he should concentrate attention on the inner world of his mind and seek by intuition to realize its true nature. If thoughts would arise, he should not become attached to them, nor should he seek to eject them, but he should let them pass unheeded, and continue his effort not to let them again arise.

Gradually attaining tranquillization, he will unconsciously enter into the more receptive state of Samadhi and in that state prejudices and hindrances will vanish, faith will be awakened, aspiration will be strengthened, and realization will be attained. But to those who are doubtful, sacrilegious, destitute of faith, encumbered with hindrances of karma, arrogance, and indolence, the door is closed.

5. To those who earnestly, faithfully and perseveringly practise Dhyana, certain benefits will accrue, but if the disciple is trained only the cessation of thought, his mind will easily sink into stupidity and he will become

self-centered and he will no longer take pleasure in doing good deeds and he will forget to be sympathetic and compassionate, therefore he should constantly discipline himself in concentration of mind on the emptiness of aspect of all things.

This will awaken in the mind of every earnest disciple a deep compassion for the sufferings of all beings and will prompt him to be dauntless, earnest and devoted. It will prompt him as far as his strength and mind permit, to practise those deeds which are beneficial to both himself and others:—Whether moving, standing, sitting he should assiduously concentrate his mind on what should be wisely done and what should be wisely left undone. This is the active side of Dhyana.

6. But if a disciple only practises the active aspect, his mind may lack tranquillity and become too susceptible to doubt and uncertainty. His mind may become out of accord with truth, or it may not attain to the highest wisdom, therefore the two aspects of cessation and activity should be practised side by side.

Cessation and activity are not antagonistic but are complementary to each other. If either one or the other is missing or out of balance the disciple will be unable to attain highest perfect wisdom. But when Dhyana is rightly practised, faith will be strengthened, insight will be cleared, and the assurance of ultimate success will become unshakable, and in due course will eventuate in self-realization of Noble wisdom.

V

SACRED APHORISMS

1. " He abused me, he laughed at me, he struck me. "
Thus one thinks and so long as he cherishes such thoughts
his anger continues.   Anger will never disappear so long
as thoughts of resentment are cherished in the mind.
Anger will disappear just as soon as thoughts of resentment are forgotten.

If the roof is improperly made or is in disrepair,
the rain will get into the house; so greed enters the mind
that is improperly trained or is out of control.

To be idle is a short road to death and to be diligent
is a way of life; foolsh people are idle, wise people are
diligent.

An arrow-maker tries to make his arrows straight;
so a wise man tries to keep his mind straight.

A disturbed mind is forever active, jumping hither
and thither, and is hard to control; but a tranquil mind
is peaceful, therefore it is wise to keep the mind under
control.

It is a man's own mind that lures him into evil ways;
it is not his enemy or his foes.

The one who protects his mind from greed, anger
and infatuation, is the one who enjoys real and lasting
peace.

2. To utter pleasant words without practising a good
life, is like a fine flower without fragrance.

The fragrance of a flower does not come to one against the wind; but honor comes to a good man even in the face of adversity.

A night seems long to a sleepless man and a journey seems long to a weary traveler; so the times of delusion and suffering seem long to a man who does not know the right teaching.

On a trail a man should travel with a companion of equal mind or one who has a better mind; one had better travel alone than to travel with a foolish man.

An insincere and evil friend is more to be feared than a wild beast; a wild beast may wound your body, but an evil friend will wound your mind.

So long as a man can not control his own mind, how can he get any satisfaction from thinking such thoughts as, " This is my son, " or " This is my treasure "? A foolish man suffers from such thoughts.

To be foolish and to recognise that one is fool, is better than to be foolish and imagine that one is wise.

A foolish man, though he associates with a wise man, cannot understand the wise man's wisdom. No more can a spoon taste of the food it carries.

Fresh milk is often slow to curdle, so sinful actions do not always bring immediate punishment. Sinful actions are more like coals of fire that are hidden in the ashes and keep on smouldering and later cause a greater fire.

A man is foolish to cherish desires for privileges and promotion and profits and honor, for such desires can never bring happiness but will rather bring suffering.

A good friend who points out mistakes and imperfections and rebukes evil is to be more respected than though he revealed a secret of hidden treasure.

3.   A man who is pleased when he receives good instruction will sleep peacefully, because his mind is cleansed thereby.

A carpenter seeks to make his beam straight; an arrowmaker seeks to make his arrow well balanced; the digger of an irrigation ditch seeks to make the water run smooth; so a wise man seeks to control his mind so that it will function smoothly and truly.

A great rock is not disturbed by the wind; neither is the mind of a wise man disturbed by either honor or abuse.

To control oneself is better than to control others; to conquer oneself is a greater victory than to conquer thousands in a battle.

To live a single day and hear a good teaching is better than to live a hundred years in ignorance.

Those who love themselves must be on constant guard lest they yield to evil desires.   Once in a lifetime, at least, they should awaken faith, either in youth, or in middle age, or even in old age.

The world is always burning, burning with fires of greed, anger and foolishness; one should flee from such a danger.

The world is like a bubble, it is like the gossamer

web of a spider, it is like the defilement of a dirty jar;
one should constantly protect the purity of his true mind.

To avoid evil, to seek the good, to keep the mind
pure; this is the essence of the Buddha's teaching.

Endurance is the most difficult of all disciplines, but
it is to the one who endures that the final victory is
given.

One must remove resentment while he is exposed
to resentment; one must remove sorrow while he is in
the midst of sorrow; one must remove greediness while
he is still tempted to be greedy.   To live a pure unselfish
life, one must live in the midst of abundance but count
nothing as his own.

To be healthy is a great advantage; to be contented
with what one has is more than the possession of great
wealth; to be considered reliable is the truest mark of
friendliness; to attain enlightenment is the highest happiness.

When one has feelings of dislike for evil, when one
feels tranquil, when one finds pleasure in listening to good
teachings;—when one has these feelings, and understands
them, he is free of fear.

Do not become attached to the things you like, do
not cherish aversion to the things you dislike.   Sorrow,
fear and bondage follow one's likes and dislikes.

5. Rust being born of iron destroys iron; so evil being
born of man destroys man.

A scripture that is not read with sincerity soon becomes covered with dust; a house that is not occupied soon becomes filthy; so an idle man soon becomes defiled.

Impure acts defile a woman; stinginess defiles charity; so evil acts defile not only this life but following lives.

But the defilement to be most dreaded is the defilement of ignorance. A man can not hope to purify either his body or mind until ignorance is removed.

It is easy to slip into shamelessness, to be pert and bold like a crow, to hurt others and then forget it; it is hard, indeed, to be ashamed, to be respected and honored to get rid of all attachments, to keep pure in thought and deed, to become wise.

It is easy to point out the mistakes of others, it is hard to admit one's own mistakes. A man broadcasts the sins of others without thinking, but he hides his own sins as a gambler hides his false dice.

The sky holds no trace of bird or smoke or storm; an evil teaching carries no enlightenment; nothing has stability; so an enlightened mind is undisturbed.

6. As a knight guards his castle gate, so one must guard his mind from dangers without and dangers within; he must not neglect it for a moment.

Oneself is master of himself, oneself is relied upon by himself, therefore, one should be thoughtful of himself and control himself.

The first step toward spiritual freedom is to control the mind, to stop idle chatter, to keep silent.

The sun makes the day bright, the moon makes the

night beautiful, a uniform adds to the dignity of a soldier; so the habit of meditation distinguishes the seeker for enlightenment.

He who is unable to guard his five senses and who becomes tempted by his surroundings, is not the one who can train for enlightenment. He who firmly guards the gateways of his five senses and who keeps his mind under control is the one who can successfully train for enlightenment.

7. He who is in bondage to his likes and dislikes can not rightly understand the singnificance of circumstances and tends to be overcome by them; he who is free from attachments rightly understands circumstances and to him all things become new and significant.

Happiness follows sorrow, sorrow follows happiness, but when one no longer discriminates happiness and sorrow, the difference between a good deed and a bad deed disappears and one is able to realize freedom.

To worry in anticipation or to cherish regret for the past is like cutting reeds that wither in a day.

The secret of health for both mind and body is not to mourn for the past, not to worry about the future, not to anticipate the future, but to live the present moment wisely and earnestly.

Do not dwell in the past, do not dream of the future, concentrate the mind on the present moment. It is a worthy task to do the present duty well and to complete it; do not seek to avoid it, do not postpone it lightly.

8.   One must try to escape from the darkness of ignorance and suffering, and must seek for enlightenemt.   In this effort and search, wisdom is the best guide and faith is the best companion.

If one's body and mind is under control he should give evidence of it in virtuous deeds.   This is a sacred duty.   Faith will then be his wealth, sincerity will give life a sweet savor, and to accumulate virtues will be his sacred task.

On the journey of life faith is nourishment, virtuous deeds are a shelter; wisdom is its light by day and right mindfulness is its protection by night.   If a man lives a pure life nothing can destroy him; if he has conquered greed nothing can limit his freedom.

One should forget himself for the sake of his family; one should forget his family for the sake of his village; one should forget all the world for the sake of enlightenment.

Everything is changeable, everything appears and disappears; there is no blissful peace until one passes beyond both life and extinction.

SECTION FOUR

THE FELLOWSHIP OF BELIEVERS

CHAPTER ONE

DUTIES OF THE BROTHERHOOD

I
HOMELESS BROTHERS

1. A man who wishes to become my disciple must be willing to give up all direct relations with his family, with the social life of the world and all dependence upon wealth. A man who has given up all such relations for the sake of the Dharma and has no abiding place for either his body or his mind has become my disciple and is to be called the homeless brother.

Though his feet leave their imprints in my footsteps and his hands carry my garment, if his mind is disturbed by greed, he is far from me. Though he dresses like a monk, but does not accept the teaching, he does not see me. But if he has removed all greed and his mind is pure and peaceful, he is very close to me though he be thousands of miles away. If he receives the Dharma he sees me in the Dharma.

2. My disciples, the homeless brothers, observe four rules and about them build their lives. First, they wear old and cast-off garments; second, they get their food by faith; third, their home is where night finds them; fourth, they use the special medicine laid down by the

brotherhood.

To carry a bowl in hand and go from house to house is a beggar's life, but he is not compelled to do it by others, he is not forced into it by circumstances or by temptation, he does it of his own free will because he thinks that a life of faith will keep him away from the delusions of life, will help him to avoid suffering, and will lead him toward enlightenment.

The life of a homeless brother is not an easy life; one ought not to undertake it if he can not keep his mind free from greed and anger, and if he can not control his mind and his five senses.

3. To believe oneself to be a homeless brother and to be able to answer when he is asked about it, one must be able to say:—"I am willing to undertake whatever is necessary to be a homeless brother. I will be sincere about it and will try to accomplish the purpose for becoming one. I will be grateful to those who help me by donations and will try to make them happy by my earnestness and good life."

To be a homeless brother one must train himself in many ways:—He must be sensitive to shame and dishonor when he fails: he must keep his body, lips and mind pure if his life is to be pure; he must guard the gates of the five senses; he must not lose control of his mind for the sake of some passing pleasure; and he must not praise himself nor rebuke others; and he must not be idle nor given to mush sleep.

In the evening he should have a time for quiet sitting and meditation and a little walk before retiring. For peaceful sleep he should rest on the right side with his feet together and his last thought should be of the time when he wishes to rise in the early morning. In the early morning he should have another time for quiet sitting and meditation and a little walk after it. During the day he should always maintain an alert mind keeping both body and mind under control, resisting all tendency to greed, anger, laziness, sleepiness, inattention, regret and suspicion, and all worldly desires. Thus, with concentrated mind, he should radiate excellent wisdom and aim at perfect enlightenment only.

4. If a homeless brother, forgetting himself, lapses into greed, gives way to anger, cherishes resentment, jealousy, conceit, self-praise, or insincerity, he is carrying a keen two-edged sword only covered by a thin cloth. One is not a homeless brother simply because he wears a monk's rags and carries a begging bowl; he is not a homeless brother just because he recites scriptures glibly; he is only a man of straw. Even if his intention is honest, if he can not control his worldly desires, he is not a homeless brother, no more than an infant is. Only those who are able to concentrate and control the mind, who manifest wisdom, who have removed all worldly desires, and whose only purpose is to attain enlightenment, only these can be called a true homeless brother.

A true homeless brother determines to reach his

goal of enlightenment even though he loses his last drop
of blood and his bones crumble into powder. Such a
one, trying his best, will finally attain the goal of a homeless brother and give evidence of it by his ability to do the
meritorious deeds of a homeless brother.

5.   The mission of the homeless brother is to carry forward the light of the Dharma.   He must preach to everybody, he must wake up sleeping people, he must correct
false ideas, he must give people a right view-point; he
must not wait for people to come to him, he must go
everywhere risking his own life even to do so.

The mission of a homeless brother is not an easy
one, so he who aspires to it should wear Buddha's clothes,
sit on Buddha's seat and enter into Buddha's room.
To wear Buddha's clothes maens to be humble and to
practise endurance: To sit on Buddha's seat means, to
see everything as emptiness, to have no abiding place,
no attachments; to enter into Buddha's room means,
to share his all-embracing compassion, to have sympathy
with everybody.   To be able to enter into Buddha's
all-embracing compassion, one must sit on Buddha's
seat of emptiness, must wear his garment of humility,
and must patiently teach all people.

6.   Those who wish to teach the Buddha's Dharma
acceptably must be concerned about four things:—First,
he must be concerned about his own behavior; second,
he must be concerned about the people he will approach

and teach what words he will use; third, he must be concerned about his motive for teaching and the end he wishes to accomplish; fourth, he must be concerned about the great compassion of Buddha.

To be a good teacher of the Dharma, first of all, a homeless brother must have his feet well set on the ground of endurance, he must be modest, he must not be eccentric or desire publicity, he must constantly think of the emptiness aspect of things, he must avoid thinking of things as this good and that bad, as this easy and that hard, he must not become attached to anything. If he is thus concerned, he will be able to behave well.

Secondly, he must exercise caution in approaching people and situations. He must avoid people who are living evil lives or people of authority; he must avoid women. Then he must approach people in a friendly way; he must always remember that things rise from a combination of causes and conditions, and standing at that point, he must not blame people, or abuse them, or speak of their mistakes, or hold them in light esteem.

Thirdly, he must keep his mind peaceful, considering Buddha as his spiritual father, considering other homeless brothers who are training for enlightenment as his teachers, look upon everybody with great compassion and then teach anybody with friendly patience.

Fourthly, he must let his spirit of compassion have free course, even as Buddha did, unto the uttermost. Especially he should let his spirit of compassion flow out to those who do not know enough to want to be enlightened.   He should wish that they might want to be enlightened, and then he should follow his wishes with an unselfish effort to awaken their interest.

II
LAY MEMBERS

1.   It has already been explained that to become a disciple of Buddha one must believe in the three treasures:—Buddha, Dharma, and the Brotherhood. To become a lay member one must have an unshaken faith in Buddha, must believe in his teachings and study them and put them into practice, and must cherish the brotherhood. To cherish the brotherhood means, to feel themselves a part of its fellowship, honoring and sustaining the homeless brothers, making regular donations for their support, and seeking their instruction.

Lay mambers should follow the five precepts for good behavior:—not to harm any sentient life, not to steal, to live a pure and restrained life, not to lie or deceive, and not to use intoxicants.

Lay members should not only believe in the teachings and study themselves, but they should, as far as they are able, explain them to others, especially to their relatives and friends, trying to awaken in them a similar faith in Buddha, Dharma and the Brotherhood, so that they too may share in Buddha's mercy.

Lay members should always keep in mind that the reason why they believe in the three treasures and why they keep the precepts is to enable them ultimately to attain enlightenment and for that reason they should avoid becoming attached to worldly disires while still living in the world of desire.

Lay members should always keep in mind that sooner or later they will be obliged to leave their parents and families and pass away from this life of birth and death, therefore, they should not become attached to things of this life but should set their minds on the world of enlightenment wherein nothing passes away.

2.   Lay members should awaken an earnest undisturbed faith in Buddha's teachings and as far as they do this they will realise within their minds a quiet and undisturbed happiness, that will shine out on all their surroundings and be reflected back to them.   This mind of faith is pure and gentle, always patient and enduring, never argues, never causes suffering to others, always keeps in mind the three treasures,—Buddha, Dharma and the Brotherhood.

Since by faith you are resting in the bosom of Buddha, you are kept far away from a selfish mind and from attachment to your possessions.   You will have no fear about your future support and no fear that anyone will harm you.   Since you have faith in the truth and the holiness of the Dharma, you can express your thoughts freely and without fear.   Since you have faith in Buddha's Pure Land, you need have no fear of death.

Since your mind is filled with compassion for all

people, you will make no distinctions among them but will treat all alike, and since your mind is free from likes and dislikes it will be pure and equitable, happy to do any good deed.

Whether you live in adversity or in prosperity will make no difference to the increase of your faith. If you cherish humility, if you respect Buddha's teachings, if you are consistent in speech and action, if you are guided by wisdom, if your mind is as resistant as a mountain, then you will make steady progress on the path to enlightenment. And though you are forced to live in a difficult situation and among people of impure minds, if you cherish faith in Buddha you can lead them toward better deeds.

3. Therefore, everyone should make the wish to hear Buddha's teaching the paramount wish of his heart. If anyone should tell him that it would be necessary to go through fire to gain enlightenment then he should be willing to pass through fire. There is a satisfaction in hearing the Buddha's name that is worth passing through a world filled with fire to gain.

If one wishes to follow the Buddha's teaching he must not be egoistic nor self-willed, but should cherish feelings of good-will toward all alike, he should respect those who are worthy of respect, he should serve those who are worthy of service and treat all others with uniform kindness. After this manner lay members are to train their own minds first and not be disturbed as to

how other people act. In this manner they are to receive
the Buddha's teaching and put it into practice, not envying
other people, not being influenced by other teachings,
not considering other ways.

Those who do not believe in Buddha's teaching have
a narrow vision and consequently a disturbed mind.
But those who believe in Buddha's teaching believe that
there is a great wisdom and a great compassion encompas-
sing everything and in that faith they are undisturbed
by trifles.

4. Those who hear and receive the Dharma know that
their lives are transient and that their bodies are merely
aggregations of sufferings and the source of all evil, so
they do not become attached to them. At the same time
they do not neglect to take good care of their bodies,
not because they wish to enjoy the physical life of the
body, but because the body is necessary for the attainment
of wisdom and for their mission of explaining the Dharma.
If they do not take good care of their bodies they can not
live long. If they do not keep well and live long, they
can not practise the Dharma personally nor explain it
to others.

If a man wishes to cross a river he is very careful
of his raft. If he has a long journey to make he takes
good care of his horse. So if a man wishes to attain
enlightenment he takes good care of his body.

Those who are disciples of Buddha must wear suitable clothing to protect the body from the extremes of

heat and cold and to hide its shame, but they should not wear them for decoration. They must eat suitable food to nourish the body so that they may hear and receive and explain the Dharma, but they should not eat for mere enjoyment. They must live in houses of enlightenment to be protected from the thieves of worldy passion and from the storms of evil teaching, but they should use the house for its real purpose and not for display or the concealment of selfish practices.

Thus you should value things and use them solely in their relation to enlightenment and the Dharma. You should not become attached to them for selfish reasons but only as they serve a useful purpose in carrying the Dharma to others. Therefore, your mind should dwell on the Dharma even when you are living with your family. You should care for them with a wise and sympathetic mind, seeking to awaken faith in their minds by many methods.

5. Lay members of Buddha's brotherhood should study the following lessons every day:—How to serve their parents, how to live with wife and children, how to control oneself, how to manifest Buddha.

To best serve parents they must learn to practise kindness toward all animate life. To live with wife and children happily they must keep away from lust and thoughts of selfish comfort. While hearing the music of the family life they must not forget the sweeter music of the Dharma, and while living in the shelter of the home, they should often seek the safer shelter of Dhyana practice where wise men find refuge from all impurity and all disturbance.

When laymen are bestowing charity they should remove all greed from their own hearts; when they are in the midst of a crowd, their minds should be in the company of wise men; when they face misfortune, they should keep the mind tranquil and free from hindrances. When they take refuge in Buddha, their desire should be for his wisdom; when they take refuge in the Dharma, their desire should be to realise its truth which is like a great ocean of wisdom; when they take refuge in the Brotherhood, their desire should be to share its peaceful fellowship unobstructed by any selfish interests.

When they wear clothes they must not forget to put on also the garment of goodness and humility. When they take an injection, they must wish to discharge all greed, anger and foolishness of mind. When they are toiling on an up-hill road, they should think of it as the road to enlightenment that will carry them beyond the world of delusion. When they are following an easy road, they should guard the mind against sloth and pride and should take advantage of its easier conditions to make a greater progress toward Buddhahood.

When they see a bridge, they must wish to tell people of the bridge of the Dharma; when they meet a sorrowful man, they should have feelings of hatred for the bitterness of this ever changing world; when they see a greedy man, they should have a great longing to keep free from the illusions of this life and to share in the true riches of enlightenment; when they see savory food, they must be on guard; when they see distasteful food, they should wish that greed might never return.

During the intense heat of summer, they must wish to be away from the heat of worldly desires and gain the fresh coolness of enlightenment. During the unbearable cold of winter, they must think of the warmth of Buddha's great compassion. When they recite the sacred scriptures, they must try not to forget them and must be very earnest to put their teaching into practice. When they think of Buddha, they must cherish a deep wish to have eyes like Buddha. As they fall asleep at night they should wish that their body, lips and mind might be purified and refreshed; when they awake in the morning, their first wish should be that during that day their minds might be clear to understand everything.

6. Laymen, although understanding that everything is characterised by " emptiness," do not treat the things that enter into a man's life lightly, but they receive them for what they are and then try to make them fit for enlightenment. Layman must not think that the world of man's life is meaningless and filled with confusion, while the world of enlightenment is full of meaning and peaceful. Rather, they should taste the way of enlightenment in all the affairs of the world. If one looks upon the world with eyes dimmed by ignorance, he will see it filled with error, but if he looks upon it with clear wis-

dom, he will see it as the world of enlightenment itself.

The fact is, there is only one world,—there are not two worlds, one meaningless and the other full of meaning, one good the other bad—People think there are two worlds by the activities of their own minds. If they could get rid of these false judgments and keep their minds pure with the light of wisdom, then they would see only one world and that world bathed in the light of wisdom.

7. Laymen who believe in Buddha taste this universal purity of oneness in everything, and in that mind they feel compassion for everyone and humble desire to serve them. Therefore, laymen should cleanse their minds from all proudness and cherish minds of humility and courtesy and service. Their minds should be like the fruitful earth that nourishes everything without partiality, that serves without complain, that endures patiently, that is always zealous, that finds its highest joy in serving all poor people by planting in their minds the seeds of Buddha's Dharma.

Thus the mind that has compassion on poor people, becomes a mother to all people, honors all people, looks upon all people as his personal friends, respects them as though they were his parents.   Therefore, though thousands of people have hard feelings and cherish ill-will toward lay believers, they can do them no harm, for what harm is a drop of poison in the waters of an ocean?

8. A lay member will add to his happiness by habits of recollection and reflection and thanksgiving. He will come to realise that his faith is Buddha's compassion itself, that it is one thing, and that it has been given to him as a present by Buddha.

There are no seeds of faith in the mud of worldly passion, but seeds of faith may be sown there because of Buddha's compassion and they will purify the mind until it has faith to believe in Buddha.

As has been said, the fragrant Candana can not grow in the forest of Eranda. In like manner the seeds of faith in Buddha can not grow in the bosom of delusion. But actually the flower of joy is blooming there, so we must conclude that while its blossoms are in the bosom of delusion, its roots are elsewhere, namely, its roots are in the bosom of Buddha, or in other words, faith in Buddha is the gift of Buddha.

If a lay believer is later carried away by self-pride, he will become jealous, envious, hateful and harmful, because his mind has again become defiled with greed, anger and foolish infatuation, but if he return to Buddha, he will accomplish an even greater service for Buddha. It is, indeed, a marvel.

CHAPTER TWO

PRACTICAL GUIDE TO TRUE LIVING

I

IN HOME AND FAMILY LIFE

1. It is a mistake to think that misfortunes come from the east or from the west; they originate within one's own mind. Therefore, it is foolish to guard against misfortunes from without and to leave the inner mind uncontrolled.

There is a custom that has come down from ancient times that ignorant people still follow. When they get up in the morning, they first wash the face and rinse the mouth, and then they bow in the six directions—to the east, west, south, north, above and below—wishing that no misfortune may come to them from any direction and that they may have a peaceful day. But it is different in the Buddha's teaching. Buddha teaches that we are to pay respect to the six directions of Truth and then that we are to behave wisely and virtuously and thus prevent all misfortune.

To guard the gates in these six directions, they are to remove the defilement of the " four deeds," control the " four evil minds," and plug the " six holes " which cause the loss of wealth.

The defilement of the " four deeds " means, killing, stealing, impurity and falsehood. The " four evil minds " are greed, anger, foolishness and fear. The " six holes " which cause the loss of wealth are the desire for intoxicating drinks, and foolish behavior, staying up late at night and losing the mind in frivolity, going to musical entertainments and shows, gambling, associating with evil companions, and neglecting word. By removing these four defilements, avoiding these four evil states of mind, and plugging these six holes of waste, the disciples of Buddha salute the six directions.

Now, what are these six directions of Truth? They are east for the way of father and son, south for the way of teacher and pupil, west for the way of husband and wife, north for the way of a man and his friend, below for the way of master and servant, and above for the way of the disciples of Buddha. A son should honor his parents and do for them all that he is supposed to do. He should wait on them, help them at their labor, cherish the family honor, protect the family property, and keep a festival in their memory after they have passed away. The parents should do five things for their children:—avoid doing anything evil, set an example of good deeds, give them an education, arrange for their marriage, and let them inherit the wealth at the proper time. If the parents and son follow this rule the family will always live happily.

A pupil should always rise when his teacher enters, should wait upon him, attend to his instructions, not neglect an offering for him, listen respectfully to his teaching. At the same time, a teacher should act rightly before a pupil, and set him a good example; he should pass on the teaching which he has learned, correctly, he should use good methods and try to prepare the pupil for honors, and he should not forget to protect the pupil from evil in every possible way. If a teacher and pupil observe this rule; their association will progress smoothly.

A husband should treat his wife with respect, courtesy and chastity. He should leave the housekeeping to her, and give her proper ornaments. At the same time, a wife should take pains with the housekeeping, manage the servants wisely, maintain her virtue as a good wife should. She should not waste her husband's income, should manage the house properly, and speak gently. If this rule is followed, it will be a happy home and there will be no quarrelling.

The rule of friendship means there should be mutual sympathy, each supplying what the other lacks and trying to benefit each other, always using friendly and sincere words. If one has a friend he should protect him from falling into evil ways, he should protect his property and wealth, should help him in his troubles, if he has misfortune give him a helping hand even supporting his family if necessary. In this way friendship will be conserved and friends will be increasingly happy together.

A master in his dealings with a servant should observe five things:—He should assign work that is suitable for his abilities, give him proper compensation, care for him if he is sick, share pleasant things with him, and give him needed rest.   Then a servant should observe five things:—He should get up in the morning before the master and go to bed after him, he should always be honest, take pains to do his work well, and try not to bring discredit to his master's name.   If these things are observed, there will be no controversy between master and servant.

A disciple should see to it that his family observe the teachings of Buddha.   Especially should they cherish respect and consideration for their Buddhist teacher. They should treat him with courtesy, attend to and observe his instructions, and always have an offering for him.   Then the teacher of Buddha's Dharma should rightly understand the teaching, rejecting wrong interpretations, emphasizing the right, and should seek to lead believers along a smooth path.   If a family follow this course, keeping the true teaching for its center, it will thrive happily.

To bow in the six directions does not mean that one does it to escape misfortunes coming from without; it means that one purposes to be on his guard in the six directions and thus to prevent evils arising within his own mind.

2.   A man should distinguish among his acquaintances those with thom he should associate and those with whom he should not associate.   The ones with whom a man should not associate are those who are lustful, clever

talkers, flatterers and wasters. The ones with whom he may associate are those who are helpful, who are willing to share happiness as well as suffering, who give good advice and who have a sympathetic nature.

A true friend, the one with whom a man may safely associate, will always advise sticking closely to the right way, will worry secretly about his friends' welfare, will console him in misfortune, will offer him a helping hand when he needs it, and will always give him good advice. It is very hard to find a friend like this, but one should try very hard to be a friend like this. As the sun warms the fruitful earth, so a good friend stimulates a man.

3. It is impossible for a son to repay his parents for their gracious kindness, even if he carried his father on his right shoulder and his mother on his left shoulder. And even if he should bathe the bodies of his parents in sweet-smelling ointments for many years, and serve his parents as an ideal son would, and gain a throne for them, and give them all the luxuries of the world, still he could not repay them for what they have done for him.

But if he leads his parents to Buddha and explains Buddha's teachings to them, and persuades them to give up a wrong course and follow a right one, and leads them to give up all greediness and to enjoy and be grateful for Buddha's mercy, that is the only possible way for him to repay his parents. Or perhaps it is more than repaying them.

Buddha's providence abides in the home where the parents are held in respect. Indeed, the parents are Buddha's providence.

4. A family is a place where a mind lives with other minds. If these minds love each other the home will be as beautiful as a flower garden. But if these minds get out of harmony with each other it is like a storm that plays havoc with a garden. If discord arises within one's family, one should not blame others but should examine his own mind and follow a right path.

Once there was a young man of deep faith. His father died when he was young but he lived happily with his mother, and then married. At first they loved happily together and then, because of a little misunderstanding, the wife and her mother-in-law came to dislike each other. This dislike went from bad to worse until finally the mother left the young couple and went off to live by herself. After the mother-in-law left, a son was born to the young couple. A report reached the mother-in-law that the young wife had said, " His mother was always nagging me and as long as she lived with us nothing pleasant ever happened, but as soon as she went we had this happy event." This angered the mother-in-law and she exclaimed, " If they chase the husband's mother from the house and a happy event takes place, then things have come to a pretty pass. Rightness must have disappeared from the world." Then she shouted, " Now we must have a funeral of this ' rightness '." Then like an insane woman the mother went to the cemetery to hold a funeral service.

The god hearing of this incident appeared in front of the insane woman and tried to reason with her, but in vain. Then the god said to her, " Then I must burn the child and its mother to death to satisfy you. But will that satisfy you ?"

Hearing this, the mother-in-law realised her mistake and apologised for her anger, and begged the god to save the life of the child. At the same time the young wife and her husband realised their injustice to the mother-in-law and sought her in the cemetery. The god reconciled them and thereafter they lived together a happy family.

Rightness is never lost forever unless one casts it away. Rightness occasionally may seem to disappear but, in fact, it never quite disappears. When it seems to be disappearing, it is because one is losing the rightness of his own mind. Two discordant minds often bring disaster. A trifling misunderstanding may be followed by great misfortune. This is especially to be feared in family life.

5. In family life the question as to how the daily expense is to be met is always uppermost. Every member must work like ants and be as diligent as bees. No one must rely upon the industry of others nor expect their charity. On the other hand, one must not consider that what he has earned is totally his own. Some of it

must be shared with others, some of it must be saved for an emergency, and some of it must be set apart for the needs of the community and the nation, and some of it must be devoted to the needs of the religious teachers. One should always remember that nothing in the world can strictly be called " mine." What comes to a person comes to him because of a combination of causes; it can be kept by him only temporarily, therefore, one must not use it selfishly or for unworthy purposes.

When Syamavati, the queen-consort of King Udayana, offered Ananda five hundred garments, Ananda received them with great satisfaction. The King, hearing of it, suspected Ananda of dishonesty, so he came to Ananda and made enquiries as to what he was going to do with the garments. Ananda replied:—" The garments of many of the brothers are in rags; I am going to distribute the garments among them."

" What will you do with the old garments? "

" We will make bed-covers out of them."

" What will you do with the old bed-covers? "

" We will make pillow-cases."

" What will you do with the old pillow-cases? "

" We will make floor covers out of them."

" What will you do with the old floor-covers? "

" We will use them for wiping cloths."

" What will you do with the old wiping cloths? "

" We will use them for floor-mops "

" What will you do with the old mops? "

" Your Highness, we will tear them in pieces and

mix them with mud and use the mud to plaster the house-walls."

Every article entrusted to us must be used with good care in some useful way, because it is not " ours " but is only entrusted to us temporarily.

II
IN THE LIFE OF WOMEN

1. There are four different types of women:—First, there are those who become angry for slight causes, who have changeable minds, who are greedy, jealous of others' happiness, and who have no sympathy for the needs of others. Second, there are those who grow angry over ordinary affairs, who are fickle and greedy, but who do not envy others their happiness and who are sympathetic for the needs of others. Third, there are those who are more broad-minded and who do not become angry very often, and who know how to control a greedy mind, but who are not able to avoid feelings of jealousy and who are not sympathetic. Fourth, there are those who are broad-minded, who can restrain feelings of greed and retain a calm mind, who do not envy others their happiness, and who are sympathetic for the needs of others.

2. When a young woman marries she should make the following resolutions: " I must honor the parents of my husband. They have given us all the advantages we have and are our wise protectors, so I must serve them

with appreciation and be ready to help them whenever
I can."

" I must be respectful to my husband's teacher
because he has given my husband a sacred teaching and
we could not live as human beings without the guidance
of the sacred teachings."

" I must cultivate my mind so that I will be able
to understand my husband and be able to help him in
his work. I must never be indifferent to my husband's
interests, thinking they are his affairs and not mine."

" I just study the nature, ability and tastes of the
family and of the servants so that I can conserve the income of my husband and not waste it."

3. The relation of husband and wife was not designed
merely for their convenience. It has a deeper significance
than the mere association of two bodies in one house.
A husband and wife should take advantage of the intima-
cies of their association to help each other train their
minds in some holy teaching and thus to mutually profit
by their marriage.

An old couple, the " ideal couple " as they were called,
once came to Buddha and said, " Lord, we married
after being acquainted from childhood and there has
never been a cloud on our happiness. Please tell us if
we can be married in the next life ? "

The Buddha gave them the wise answer:—" If you
both have exactly the same faith, if you both receive the
same teaching in exactly the same way, and if you have

the same wisdom, then you will have the same mind in the next birth."

4. The young wife of the eldest son of the rich merchant, Anathapindada, was proud and arrogant and did not listen to the instruction of her husband and his parents and consequently there was trouble in the family. One day the Blessed One came to visit Anathapindada and noticed it. He called her to him and spoke to her kindly, saying, " There are seven types of wives, namely, a wife who is like a murderer. She has an impure mind, does not honor her husband and then loses her heart to another man. Second, a wife who is like a thief. She never considers her husband's labor but thinks only of her desire for luxury. She wastes her husband's income to satisfy her appetite and by so doing steals from him. Third, a wife who is like a master. She rails at her husband, neglects the house-keeping and thinks ony of her own comfort. Fourth, a wife who is like a mother. She cares for her husband as though he were a child, she protects her husband as a mother does her son, and she looks after his income as though he was incapable of doing so. Fifth, a wife who is like a sister. She is faithful to her husband and serves him like a sister with modesty and reserve. Sixth, a wife who is like a friend. She tries to please her husband like a friend who has just returned from a long absence. She is modest, behaves nicely and treats her husband with great respect. Seventh, a wife who is like a maid-servant. She serves her husband

well and with fidelity. She respects him, obeys his commands, has no wishes of her own, no ill-feeling, no resentment, and always tries to make him happy."

" My dear lady, which type of wife are you like, or would you wish to be like? "

Hearing the kind words of the Blessed One she was ashamed of her past conduct and replied that she would like to be a wife like the maid-servant. She changed her life and became her husband's helper and together they sought enlightenment.

5. Amrapali was a wealthy and famous courtezan of Vaisali and many young and beautiful girls lived with her. She called upon the Blessed One and asked him to give them some good teaching which he did, speaking as follows:—

" Amrapali, the mind of a woman is easily disturbed and is easily misled. She yields to her desires and gives up to jealousy more easily than a man does, therefore, it is harder for a woman to follow the Noble Path. This is especially true for a young and beautiful woman. But, Amrapali, you must remember that youth and beauty do not last but are followed by sickness, old age and suffering. You should decide to follow the Noble Path while you are yet young, but to do that you must overcome all desire for wealth, affection, and pleasure. Desire for wealth and love are a woman's besetting temptation, Amrapali, but they are not the eternal treasures. Enlightenment is the only treasure that holds its value.

Strength is followed by illness; youth must yield to old age; life gives way to death. One must go away from a beloved one to live with a hateful one; one may not follow the path he wishes for very long; it is the law of life. The only thing that protects one and brings one to lasting peace is enlightenment. Amrapali, you should seek enlightenment at once."

She listened to him, became his disciple and as an offering to him she gave the Brotherhood her beautiful pleasure park.

6. There is no distinction of sex on the path to enlightenment. If a woman possesses a mind to seek for enlightenment she is a heroine. Mallika, the daughter of King Prasenajit and the Queen of King Ayodhya, was such a heroine. She had great faith in the teaching of the Blessed One and uttered the ten following vows and and three great wishes, in his presence:—

"My Lord, Until I gain enlightenment (1) I will not violate the sacred precepts; (2) I will not be arrogant before people who are older than myself; (3) I will not become angry with anyone; (4) I will not be jealous of others nor envy their possessions; (5) I will not be selfish either in mind nor property; (6) I will try to make people happy with the things I receive and will not hoard them for myself; (7) I will receive all people courteously, give them what they need and will speak kindly to them; I will consider their circumstances and not my convenience; I will try to benefit them without partiality.

(8) If I see others suffering from disease or in prison, I will try to relieve their sufferings and will try to make them happy by explaining to them the reasons and the rules. (9) If I see others catching living animals and being cruel to them or violating any other law, I will punish them if they are to be punished, or teach them if they should be taught, and then I wil try to correct their mistakes. (10) I will not forget to hear the right teaching, for I know that when one neglects the right teaching he quickly falls away from the truth that abides everywhere, and will fail to reach the other shore of enlightenment."

Then she uttered the following three wishes to save poor people:—" First, I will try to make everybody peaceful. This wish, I believe, in whatever life I hereafter receive, will be a root of goodness that will grow into the wisdom of good teaching. Second, after I have received the wisdom of good teaching, I will teach all people without tiring. Third, I will protect the true teaching which I give, with my body, my property and my life."

The true significance of family life is the opportunity it gives for mutual encouragement and mutual aid on the path to enlightenment, and even an ordinary woman, if she has the same mind to seek enlightenment and utters the same vows, and wishes, may become as great a disciple as Mallika was.

III

IN SERVICE

1. There are seven teachings which lead a country to prosperity:—First, people should assemble often to discuss conditions and to provide for the national defence. Second, in the consideration of national affairs people of all social classes should meet together in unity. Third, people should respect old customs and not change them, they should observe rules of ceremony and maintain justice. Fourth, they should recognise differences of sex and seniority and family rank, thus maintaining the purity of families and society. Fifth, cherish loyalty for parents and teachers. Sixth, honor the ancestral shrines and keep up the annual festivals. Seventh, esteem public morality, honor virtuous conduct, respect virtuous teachers and make offerings to them.

If a country follows these teachings, it will prosper and will be held in respect by all other countries.

2. Once there was a King who was notably successful in ruling his kingdom. Because of his wisdom he was called King Great-Light. He explained the principles of his administration as follows:—The best method for ruling a country is to first rule oneself. A ruler should come before his people with a heart of compassion, and should first teach them and lead them to remove all impurities from their minds. The happinees that comes from good teachings far exceeds any enjoyment that the

material things of the world can offer, therefore, give the people good teaching and keep their minds and bodies in tranquillity. When poor people come to me, I open the storehouse and let them take what they want, and then I take advantage of the opportunity to teach them the wisdom of getting rid of all greed and evil.

Each man has a different view of things according to the state of his mind. Some people see this city as fine and beautiful, others see it as dirty and dilapidated. It all depends on the state of their minds. Those who hold good teachings in respect see, even in the common things of trees and stones, all the beautiful lights and colors of lapis lazuli, while greedy people who do not know enough to control their own minds are blind even to the splendor of a golden palace. Everything in the nation's daily life is like that. The mind is the sourse of everything, therefore, in my rule I first seek to have the people train their minds.

3. In wise statecraft the first principle is this principle of King Great-Light—to lead the people to train their minds. To train the mind means to seek enlightenment, therefore, the wise ruler will give his first attention to Buddha's teaching.

If a ruler has faith in Buddha, is devoted to his teachings, appreciates and pays tribute to virtuous and merciful people, there will be no favoritism toward either friends or enemies and his country will always remain prosperous. If a country is prosperous it is neither necessary to attack any other country nor does it need weapons of attack.

When people are happy and satisfied, class differences disappear, good deeds are promoted, virtues are increased, and people respect each other. Then every one becomes prosperous; the weather and temperature become normal; the sun and the moon and stars shine just right; rain and wind come timely; and all the natural evils disappear.

4. The duty of a ruler is to protect his people. The ruler of a people is the parent of his people and he protects them by his laws. He must raise his people like parents raise their children, giving them a dry cloth when they take away a wet one without waiting for the child to cry. In like manner he must remove suffering and bestow happiness without waiting for people to complain. Indeed, his statecraft is not perfect unless his people abide in peacefulness. They are his country's treasure.

Therefore, a wise ruler is ever thinking of his people and does not forget them for a moment. He thinks of their hardships, he plans for their prosperity. To rule wisely he must be advised about everything—about the water, about draught, about storm and rain; he must know about the crops, the chances of harvest, the health of his people, their comforts and their sorrows. He must be thoroughly informed as to the guiltiness of bad men, and as to the merits of good men, thus he is in position to rightly award both punishment and praise.

A wise ruler gives to his people when they are in need, as well as collects from them when they are prosperous. He should exercise good judgment when collecting taxes and make the levy as light as possible, thus keeping his people peaceful. A wise ruler will protect his people by his power and dignity. One who thus rules his people is worthy to be called a King.

5. The King of Truth is the king of kings. His ancestry is of the purest and the highest. He not only rules the four quarters of the world, he is also Lord of Wisdom and protector of all Virtuous Teachings. Wherever he goes, fightings cease and ill-will vanishes. He rules with equity by the power of Truth and by vanquishing evil he brings peace to all people.

The King of Truth never slays nor steals nor acts lasciviously. He never cheats nor abuses nor lies nor chatters idly. His mind is free from all greed, anger and foolishness. He removes these ten evils and in their place establishes the ten vitrues of kindness, generosity, purity, fidelity, appreciation, honesty, sobriety, charity, tranquillity and wisdom. Because his rule is based upon Truth he is invincible. Wherever Truth appears violence ceases and ill-will vanishes. There is no dissension among his people, therefore they dwell in quietness and safety; his mere presence brings peacefulness and happiness. That is why he is called the King of Truth, and his Kingdom the Kingdom of Truth.

Since the King of Truth is king of kings, all other

rulers praise his excellent name and rule their lesser kingdoms after his example. Thus the King of Truth is sovereign over all kings and under its righteous sway they bring safety to their people and fulfil their duties with wisdom.

6. A wise judge will temper his verdicts with compassion. He will try to consider each case with clear wisdom and then make his verdict accord with five principles: —First, he must examine into the truthfulness of the facts presented. Second, he must be sure that they fall within his jurisdiction. If he renders a judgment with full authority it is effective, but if he renders judgment without authority it only causes complications; he should wait for a right occasion. Third, he must judge justly, that is, he must enter into the mind of the defendant and if he finds that the deed was done without criminal intent, he should discharge the man. Fourth, he should pronounce his verdict with kindness and not harshness, that is, he should apply a proper punishment but should not go beyond that. A good judge will instruct a criminal with kindness and give him time to reflect upon his mistakes. Fifth, he should judge with sympathy and not in anger, that is, he should condemn the crime but not the criminal. He should let his judgment rest upon a foundation of sympathy, and he should use the occasion to try and make the criminal realise his mistakes and thus give the man an opportunity to be reborn under better conditions.

7. If an important minister of a king neglects his duties, works for his own profit, accepts bribes, it will cause the rapid decay of public morals. Other people will cheat each other, a strong man will attack a less powerful one, a noble will mistreat a commoner, a wealthy man will take advantage of the poor, there will be no justice for anyone, mischief will abound and troubles will multiply.

Under such circumstances faithful ministers will retire from public service, wise men will keep silent from fear of complications, and only flatterers will hold government positions, and they will use their political power to enrich themselves with no thought for the sufferings of the people. Under such conditions the power of the government becomes ineffective for good and its righteous policies fall in ruins. Such unjust officials are thieves of the people's happiness, and are worse than thieves because they defraud both ruler and people and are the cause of the nation's troubles. The king should root out such ministers and punish them severely.

But even in a country which is ruled by a good king and by just laws, there is another form of disloyalty that is even more to be dreaded,—the disloyalty of sons to their parents. There are sons who give themselves up to love of wife and children and who forget the grace of their parents who nursed them and cared for them during many years. They neglect their parents, rob their parents of their possessions, and neglect their teaching.

Such sons are to be counted among the worst criminals in a country. And why? Because they are disloyal to their parents whose love has been very great and was continued for many years, a love that could not be repaid if the sons honored them and treated them kindly through their life. Those who are unfaithful to rulers and unfaithful to parents should be punished as the worse of criminals.

And also, in a country which is ruled by a good king and by just laws, there is another form of disloyalty that is even worse than these,—disloyalty to religious teachers. There are people in every country who give themselves up to selfish enjoyments entirely forgetting the three treasures—Buddha, Dharma and the Brotherhood. Such people destroy their country's sanctuaries, burn the sacred scriptures, persecute the teachers of of righteousness, and violate all the sacred teachings of Buddha. Such peolpe are the country's worst enemies. And why? Because they destroy the spiritual faith of a nation, which is its foundation and the source of its virtues and prosperity. Such people by ruining the faith of others are digging their own graves.

All other sins may be counted light in comparison with these three disloyalties. These who are thus disloyal should be punished most severely.

8. It is possible there may be a conspiracy against a good king who is ruling his country wisely, or bandits may raid the country. In this case the king should adopt

three determinations. He should say to himself: First, these conspirators and bandits are threatening the good order and welfare of our country, I must protect the people and country even by employing its soldiers. Second, I will first try to find some way of controlling them without resorting to the use of soldiers. Third, I will try to capture them alive if possible, and disarm them. By adopting these three determinations the King will be proceeding most wisely.

By this procedure the country and its soldier will be encouraged by the king's wisdom and dignity and will respect both his firmness and his grace. Then if it is necessary to call upon the soldiers they will fully understand the reason for the war and what its nature is to be. Then the soldiers will enter battle with courage and loyalty, grateful for the king's wise and gracious sovereignty. Such a war will not only bring victory but will add virtue to a country.

CHAPTER THREE

BUILDING A BUDDHA LAND

I

THE HARMONY OF BROTHERHOOD

1. Let us think of a desert country lying in absolute darkness and many animals moving about in it blindly. Naturally they will be frightened and as they run into each other during the night there will be frequent fighting. Such a conception is a pitiable one. Now let us think that a superior man appears with a great light and everything becomes bright and clear. We can imagine the relief of the creatures as they are able to look about, and their happiness as they recognise each other and renew their companionship.

This is like the field of human life as it lies in the darkness of ignorance. Those who have no enlightenment wander about in loneliness and fear. They are born alone and die alone, they do not know how to associate together in peacefull harmony, and it is natural and fearful.

Suddenly Buddha appears in human form and by his wisdom and compassion illumines the world. In this light people find themselves and find others and are glad to establish human fellowship and harmonious relations.

Thousands of people may live in the world but we can not call it a fellowship until they know each other and have sympathy for each other.   A true community is a place where truth and wisdom are its light, and where the people know each other and trust each other and have things in common, and where there is a harmonious organization.   In fact, harmony is its life and its happiness and its meaning.

2.   There are, however, organizations of three kinds:— First, there are those organised on a bases of power and wealth and the authority of great leaders.   Second, there are those which are organised on a basis of convenience to the menbers, and which exist only as long as there are convenience and do not quarrel.   Third, there are those which are organised with some good teaching as the center and with harmony as its very life.   Of course the third is the only true organization, for in that organization they are living in one spirit from which unity of spirit, various kinds of virtue will arise.   In such an organization there is harmony, satisfaction and happiness.

Enlightenment is like rain that falls on a mountain and gathers into little rivulets, that run into brooks, and then into a river which increases until it flows into the ocean.   The rain of the sacred teaching falls on all people alike without regard to their conditions and circumstances. Those who accept it gather into little groups, then into communities, then into organizations, and finally become the great Ocean of Enlightenment.   Enlightened minds mix like milk and water and quickly organize into a harmonious Brotherhood.

Thus true teaching is the fundamental requirement of a perfect organization and, as mentioned above, true teaching is the light which enables people to recognise each other and to become adjusted to each other and to smooth out the rough places in their minds. Thus the organization that gathers about the perfect teachings of Buddha is an ideal organization, and its chief purpose should be to perpetuate the teachings and spirit of Buddha. They should try to persuade everybody to observe these teachings and to train their minds in accordance with them. Thus Buddha's Brotherhood will theoretically include everybody, but infact those who have the same religious faith.

3. Buddha's Brotherhood will have two classes of members:—there will be those who are teaching the members and those who are supporting the teachers, seeing that they have the needed food and clothing. Together they must try to disseminate and perpetuate the teaching. Then to make the Brotherhood perfect there must be perfect harmony between the members. It is only as the teachers love the members and the members honor the teachers, that there can be harmony and meaning and power both to give and receive the teaching.

Members of Buddha's Brotherhood should associate together with affectionate sympathy, giving and receiving the true teaching with humility and sincerity, seeking to become one in spirit.

4.   There are six things that influence the harmony of an organization:—First, sincerity of speech; second, sincerity and kindness of acts; third, sincerity and sympathy of spirit; fourth; equal sharing in a common property; fifth, following the same pure precepts; and sixth, all having right views. Among these six things,—all having right views, is, of course, the main body, all the others are merely wrappings.

Then there are seven methods to be followed if the Brotherhood is to be a success:—(1) They should gather together frequently to listen to the teachings and to discuss them. (2) Members of different social classes should mingle freely and respect each other. (3) Reverence the teaching and respect the rules and do not change them. (4) Elder and younger members are to treat each other with courtesy. (5) Let sincerity and reverence mark their spirit. (6) Purify the mind in a quiet place and offer the place to another before they take it for oneself. (7) Be sympathetic with all people, treat visitors cordially, console sickness with kindness. An organization that follows these methods will never die.

Then there are another seven rules that are valuable:—(1) Maintain a pure spirit and do not ask for troublesome things. (2) Maintain integrity and remove all greed. (3) Be patient and do not argue. (4) Keep silent and do not chatter idly. (5) Submit to the regulations and do not be overbearing. (6) Maintain an even mind and do not follow different teachings. (7) Be thrifty and saving. If members will follow these rules the Brotherhood will endure.

5. As mentioned above, a teaching organization should make harmony its very life; so an organization without harmony can not be a successful Brotherhood. Each one should be on his guard not to be the cause of discord. If discord appears, they should try to remove it as early as possible for discord will soon ruin any organization. Blood stains can not be removed by more blood; resentment can not be removed by more resentment; resentment can be removed only by forgetting it.

Once there was a king whose name was Calamity, whose country was conquered by a neighboring warlike king named Brahmadatta. King Calamity after hiding for a time was captured together with his wife, only his son the prince escaping. The prince tried to find some way of saving his father but in vain. When the day of his father's execution arrived, the prince in disguise made his way to the execution ground to witness the death of his ill-fated father. The father noticed him in the crowd and called out loudly as though talking to himself:— " Do not search for a long time; do not act in a short time, resentment can not be calmed by resentment."

Afterward the prince sought for a long time for some method of revenge. At last he was employed as an attendant in Brahmadatta's palace, and won the king's favor.   One day the king went hunting and the prince went with him and sought some opportunity for revenge. The prince was able to lead the king away from his escort into a lonely place, and the king being weary fell asleep on the lap of the prince, so fully had he come to trust the prince.   The prince drew his dagger and pointed it at the king's throat but hesitated.   The words of his father flashed into his mind and although he tried again he could not kill the king.   Suddenly the king awoke and told the prince he had had a bad dream in which the son of King Calamity was trying to kill him.   The prince hastily grasped the king and said that the time had come for him to revenge his father; still he could not do it. Suddenly he threw the dagger away and knelt in front of the king and confessed all and told him of the final words of his father.   When the king heard the prince's words and the final words of his father, he was very much impressed and forgave the prince.   Later he restored the family property to the prince and they continued to to live in friendship.

" Do not search for a long time " means that resentment should not be cherished.   " Do not act in a short time " means that friendship should not be broken hastily. Resentment can not be satisfied by resentment, it can only be gotten rid of by forgetting it.   In the fellowship of a brotherhood that is based on the harmony of right teaching, every member should understand the spirit of this tory.   But not only should members of a brotherhood understand its spirit, it is just as necessary in the daily life of evry body.

II
THE BUDDHA'S PURE LAND

1. As has been explained, if a brotherhood does not forget its duty of spreading the teachings of Buddha's Dharma and of living in harmony, the organization will steadily become larger and the teaching will spread more and more widely. This means that more and more people will be seeking enlightenment, and it also means that the evil armies of greed, anger and ignorance, which are led by that devil of ignorance, are beginning to retreat and that wisdom, light, faith and gladness, are advancing.

The devil's dominion is where there is greed, darkness, struggling, a sword, fighting and bloodshed, and also, jealousy, prejudice, hatred, cheating, flattering, fawning, secrecy and abuse. Now suppose the light of wisdom shines upon that dominion, and the rain of mercy falls upon it, and faith begins to take root, and blossoms of gladness begin to spread their fragrance, that devil's domain will turn into Buddha's Pure Land.

And just as a soft breeze and a little blossom on a branch are harbingers of spring, so because a man gets enlightenment grass, trees, and land, mountain, river and everything begin to throb with new life. If a man's mind becomes pure, his surroundings will become pure also.

2.   In a land where the true teaching prevails, every dweller has a pure and tranquil mind. Indeed, Buddha's compassion never tires of benefiting all people, and Buddha's shining spirit burns away all impurities. A pure mind soon becomes a deep mind, a mind that is commensurate with the Noble Path, a mind that loves to give, a mind that loves to keep the precepts, an enduring mind, a zealous mind, a calm mind, a wise mind, a compassionate mind, a mind that leads people to enlightenment by many and skilful ways. Thus shall the Buddha's Land be built.

A family seeks enlightenment and Buddha's providence changes its poverty into prosperity; a country that suffers because of social distinctions, by Buddha's providence is transformed into a fellowship of kindred spirits. A golden palace that is blood-stained can not be the abiding place of Buddha. A little shack where the moonlight filters through cracks in the roof, by Buddha's providence can be changed into the palace of a king, provided the mind of the master of the shack is pure.

A Buddha Land is founded and built upon the pure mind of a single man, but that single pure mind draws other kindred minds to itself in the fellowship of a brotherhood. Faith in Buddha spreads from individual to family, from family to village, from village to towns, to cities, to countries, to the whole world. Indeed, earnestness and faithfulness in teaching the Dharma is what builds every Buddha Land.

3. Indeed, when seen from one angle, the world with all its greed and injustice and bloodshed appears to be a devil's world, but as people come to believe in Buddha's enlightenment blood will be turned into milk, greed will be turned into compassion and charity and, lo, the devil's land is a Buddha Land of Purity.

It seems an impossible task to empty an ocean with a single spoon, but the determination to do it even if it takes many, many lives, is the mind with which one should receive Buddha's enlightenment. Buddha is waiting on the other shore in his world of Enlightenment wherein there is no greed, nor anger, nor ignorance, but where there is the light of wisdom and the dew of compassion. It is a land of peace, a refuge for those who suffer, a place of rest for the weary teachers of the Dharma. In this Pure Land is boundless Light and everlasting Life. Those who reach its haven will nefer return to the world of delusion but will abide in its peaceful bliss of Enlightenment. Indeed, that Pure Land where the flowers perfume the air with wisdom and the birds sing the holy Dharma, is the final destination for all mankind.

4. Though this Pure Land is the place for enjoyment it is not the place for idleness. Its beds of fragrant flowers are not for slothful idleness, but are places for refreshment and rest where one regains energy and zeal for Buddha's mission of enlightenment.

Buddha's mission is everlasting. As long as men live and creatures exist, and as long as selfish and defiled minds create their own world and circumstances, so long the children of Buddha who have crossed to the Pure Land will be zealous to return to the land from where they came. For them it will no longer be a land of delusion, but it will still be a land of suffering that calls for boundless compassion and teaching and service.

As one little candle lights another, so the light of Buddha's compassion will pass from one mind to another mind endlessly. The children of Buddha as they realise Buddha's spirit of compassion adopt Buddha's task of enlightenment and purification and thus Buddha's Land is glorified forever.

III

THOSE WHO HAVE RECEIVED GLORY IN BUDDHA'S LAND

1. Syamavati, the consort of King Udyana, was deeply devoted to Buddha. She lived, of course, in the inner courts of the palace and could not go out, but her maid Uttala, a hunchback, who had an excellent memory, used to go out and attend the Buddha's preaching. On her return she would repeat to the Queen the teachings of the Blessed One, and thus the Queen increased in wisdom and purity.

The second wife of the King was jealous of the first wife and sought to kill her. She slandered her to the King and caused the same stories to be repeated to the King from other sources until finally the King heeded them and sought to kill the first wife, Syamavati. The Queen stood in front of the King so calmly that the King had no heart to kill her and regaining control of himself he apologized to her for his distrust of her.

The jealousy of the second wife increased and she sent wicked men to set fire to the inner courts of the palace. Syamavati remained calm and quieted and encouraged the bewildered maids, and then, without fear, died peacefully in the spirit she had learned from the Blessed One, and Uttala, the hunchback died with her. Among the many women disciples of Buddha, these two are most highly honored: Queen Samavati of merciful spirit and the hunchback maid, the wise Uttala.

2. Prince Mahanama, of the Sakya clan and a cousin of the Buddha, had great faith in Buddha and was one of his most faithful followers. At that time a violent king named Virudabha of Kosala made a conquest of the Sakya clan. Prince Mahanama went to the King and begged for the lives of the prisoners, but the King would not listen to him, so he made a proposition asking the King to let as many prisoners escape as could run away while he was diving in a neighboring pond. To this the King assented, thinking that the time would be very short. The gate of the prison was opened as Mahanama dived into the water and the prisoners rushed for safety. But Mahanama did not come out of the water but sacrificed his life for the lives of his people.

3.   Utpalavaruna was a famous nun whose wisdom was compared with that of Maudgalyayana, a great disciple of Buddha. She was, indeed, a nun of the nuns and was always their leader and never tired of teaching them.

Devadatta was a very wicked and cruel man who poisoned the mind of King Ajatasatru and persuaded him to murder his own father and to turn against the teachings of Buddha.   But later King Ajatasatru repented, broke off the friendship with Devadatta and became a humble disciple of Buddha.   At the time he was repulsed from the castle gate in an attempt to see the King, he met Utpalavaruna coming out.   It made him very angry and he struck her and seriously wounded her.   She returned to her convent in great pain and when the other nuns tried to console her she said to them:—" Sisters, human life is very precious, but everything is transient and empty.   Only the world of enlightenment endures and is peaceful.   You must keep on with your training." Then she passed away.

4.   Angulimalya, once a terrible bandit, who had killed many people, was saved by the Blessed One, and he became one of the brotherhood.

One day he went into a town for begging where a short time before he had led a raid and caused much hardship and suffering.   The villagers fell upon him and beat him severely, but he went back to the Blessed One with his body still bleeding and fell at his feet and thanked him for the opportunity that had come to him to suffer for his former cruel deeds.   He said:—

"Blessed One, My name originally was 'No-killing,' but because of my ignorance I took many precious lives and from each I collected a finger, because of which I came to be called, Angulimalya, the collector of fingers! Then through your compassion I learned widsom and became devoted to the three treasures, Buddha, Dharma and Brotherhood.   When a man drives a horse or cow he has to use a whip, but you, Blessed One, purified my mind without the use of whip or rope or hook.   Today, Blessed One, I have suffered only what was my due. I do not wish to live, I do not wish to die.   I only wait for my time to come."

5. Maha-Maudgalyayana together with the venerable Sariputra were the Buddha's two greatest disciples. When the teachers of other schools saw Maudgalyayana distributing the pure water of the Buddha's teachings and saw the people eagerly drinking of it, they became jealous and applied all sorts of hindrances to his preaching. But none of the hindrances discouraged him in his teaching not prevented his teaching from spreading abroad. The followers of other schools attempted to kill him. Twice he escaped harm but the third time he was surrounded by many people and fell under their blows. Sustained by enlightenment he calmly received their blows while his flesh was torn and his bones crushed and when he died he died peacefully.

THE APPENDIX

I THE PRECEPTS OF KING ASOKA

II THE PRECEPTS OF PRINCE SHOTOKU

I THE PRECEPTS OF
KING ASOKA

I

Do not kill any creature nor offer them in religious sacrifice, in all my dominion. Do not hold ceremonial feasts for, with a few good exceptions, they lead to misbehavior and trouble.

II

My vassals must go on a pilgrimage every five years, in order to recall the following teachings:—It is a good deed to be kind to parents; it is a good deed to make offerings to friends, acquaintances, relatives and homeless holy-men; it is a good deed to refrain from slaying animals; it is a good deed to spend little and to save a little.

III

The preaching of Buddha's Dharma is the supreme need of my kingdom. Since it has been spread abroad like the sound of a great drum, for the first time in several hundred years, the non-killing of animals, kindness to relatives and homeless holy-men, respect and courtesy to parents and teachers, have increased. My son, grandson, and great grand-son are instructed to spread the teaching of the Dharma everywhere because the preaching of the Dharma promotes the most excellent behavior.

IV

It is hard to accomplish a good deed and it is easy to do an evil deed, but even if it at times seems alomst impossible, one should determine to do the good deed. A good deed only half accomplished is also evil.

V

My chief duty is to promote the public welfare. Hereafter, wherever I am and whatever I may be doing, I command my officials to make frequent reports to me regarding public affairs and the welfare of the people.

VI

Even if a man makes a munificent donation but lacks purity and self-control and faith and gratitude for favors received, he is only a common man.

VII

People are accustomed to offer many and various prayers when they suffer from sickness or other distress, but such prayers are meaningless and bring little benefit. On the other hand, a prayer for the Dharma brings great and endless benefits both in the present life and in after lives. A prayer for the Dharma is an expression of worship and devotion to his holy teaching and with it should go donations to the Homeless Brothers, honor and respect to parents and teacher, right treatment of servants and kindness to all animate life.

VIII

Any honor or praise that comes to one will benefit little unless he is devoted to the Dharma and obeys its teachings. The honor and praise which I crave must have relation to following lives, that is, I desire to avoid causing suffering or distress to anyone, knowing that it is caused by evil conduct.

IX

There is no greater donation that the gift of the Dharma; there is no greater friendship than is based upon the Dharma; there in no better relation than are caused by the Dharma. Everywhere it will be recognised and praised and people will unite in saying:—" It is a good deed; let us do the same."

X

After I had been crowned for eight years I made the conquest of Kalinga. A hundred and fifty thousand captives were brought in and a hundred thousand of them were slaughtered, besides which several times that number died in battle and from sickness. I long ago repented of that crime but still suffer extremely because of it. Afterward I became a disciple of the Dharma nad have tried to be faithful to it, honoring it and preaching it.

I now realise that a victory by the Dharma is the great victory and I have seen it accomplished again and again boty within my own kingdom and in the neighboring kingdoms. In many other countries where my authority is not recognised, they are hearing my preaching of the Dharma and are obeying it. This victory for the Dharma which is being attained everywhere is based upon gladness and brings benefits and happiness, both in the present life and following lives. The victory of the Dharma is the only ture victory. May the happiness of all people be based upon it.

XI

I firmly believe that there can be no enduring bene-fits or happiness to a country except as the people possess deep admiration for, deep understanding of, strong respect for, highest honor for, most fear of and most earnest efforts for, the Dharma. But by my teaching, faith in and admiration for the Dharma have increased day by day and, I believe, will continue to increase in the future. My subjects also obey the Dharma and live in accordance with its teachings, and those who are tempted to commit crimes are restrained by it.

XII

The Dharma inspires to good deeds. How great is the Dharma! It inspires its believers to restrain worldly passion, to act rightly, to cherish sympathy and honesty, and to purify the activities of body, lips and mind.

XIII

People frequenlty refer to their good deeds, saying, "I have done such and such a deed." But very few boast of the number and character of their evil deeds. Very few people see and recognise the bad side of their deeds. It is very difficult for people to judge fairly as to their deeds. Rampant evil, mercilessness, anger, conceit and jealousy, lead people into other and deeper wordly passions. One should recognise their evil power and determine within himself. "I will not be ruined by such things"; and seeing virtuous deeds he should say to himself, "Such good deeds lead us to benefits and happiness, both in the present life and in following lives."

XIV

Twenty years after I was crowned I went to the village of Lumbini where Buddha was born and made an offering and devotion. I erected a marble column surmounted by the image of a horse with an inscription to commemorate the place where the World-honored One was born. I exempted the village of Lumbini from taxes and only collected one eighth of the produce.

II THE PRECEPTS OF
PRINCE SHOTOKU

I

Above all things esteem harmony, and respect a non-opposing spirit. Truly wise men are few and people are often left to their own devices. For this reason, some of the people, who are not obedient to the rulers and who do not honor their parents, presently mislead the people and come in conflict with neighboring people. But if the government can bring the people together in a friendly spirit to discuss the conditions and to settle affairs, the truth will be reconised and accepted by both parties and harmony will be restored. Such a course will never fail.

II

Faithfully respect the " three treasures ": Buddha, Dharma and the Brotherhood. These three are the destination of all sentient creatures, the unmistakable truth for all nations, and the fellowship of all nations. This rule can not be neglected by any people in any world. Really bad men are very few and they can be taught and guided, but how are they to be taught and guided apart from the three treasures?

III

Respect the Imperial commands. The ruler is analogous to heaven, the subjects to the earth. The heaven covers the earth, and the earth supports heaven; if the four seasons pass smoothly, everything functions well. But if the earth tries to dominate heaven, it crumbles into powder. For this reason heaven commands and the earth receives, and for the same reason the ruler commands and the subjects should obey. Therefore, every subject should respect the Imperial commands, if not there will be confusion.

IV

The principle of courtesy is the secret of successful governing. All men of the nobility and their associates in their dealings with subjects should be sincerely courteous. Unless the governing body is courteous the people will become dissatisfied. If the people are not courteous, disorders and crime will bound. If the good order of the country is to be maintained, both the governing body and the people must maintain courtesy in all their relations. If mutual courtesy exists the country will naturally remain peaceful.

V

Magistrates should first cast aside all favoritism and selfish greed and then afterwards judge the complaints of the people. The appeals of the people may be counted a thousand in a day. If there are a thousand in a day how many will it be after many years? Thus every decision is important. Of late many magistrates are profiting by their judgements and accepting bribes. A wealthy man's appeal is like throwing a pebble into water, while a poor man's appeal is like throwing water among pebbles. For this reason a poor man has no refuge and the duty of subjects will be neglected.

VI

The governing body should discover the good deeds of the people and suitably reward them, at the same time they should expose the evil deeds and punish them. This is an ancient rule. Wicked men soon throw a country into disorder and turn upon the people like a sword to destroy them. Flatterers tell the governing body of the mistakes of the people, and then turn to tell the people of the mistakes of the governing body. Such sycophants are neither faithful to the ruler nor to the people and are the source of great disorder.

VII

Every man should have his particular duty, and he should not act beyond his duty. If a wise man is appointed to a government position praise rises on every hand, but if a crooked man is appointed complaints and troubles soon arise. There are very few people who have natural wisdom, but if any man thinks deeply he soon gains wisdom. If a suitable man gets a position, whether affairs are large or small, the country is well ruled. Whether the occasion is critical or not, if a country has a wise man, it feels easy. And because there are some wise men, country will not fall into danger forever. Therefore, in the days of old, wise kings sought for true men to fill positions of authority, but did not waste time seeking some position for a man.

VIII

All nobility and their associates should attend hearings early and retire late. Their duties are not few nor light; a long day is hardly sufficient to give them proper attention. If they are late in the morning they will be late for emergency calls, and if they retire early their duties will not have been completed.

IX

Faith is the foundation of Justice. One should have faith in everything. Right judgments as to what is good and what is evil, as to what is success and what is failure, are based upon faith. If both the ruler and the people have faith there is nothing but what can be accomplished. If the ruler and the people do not possess faith everything will fail.

X

Forget resentment, control anger. Do not become angry just because some one opposes you. Every one has a mind, and every mind comes to a decision and the decisions will not always be alike. If he is right, you are wrong; if you are not quite a saint, he is not quite an idiot. Both disputants are men of ordinary mind, who is capable of judging an argument between them? If both are wise men or both foolish men their argument is probably a circle that has no end. For this reason, if your opponent grows angry, you should give the more heed to your self lest you too are in error. One can seldom get all he wishes, it is wiser to compromise with the other man.

XI

A magistrate should try to evaluate achievements and crimes clearly and justly, and then award suitable praise and punishment. Nowadays praise is not in accord with achievement and punishment is out of proportion to crime. All magistrates should exercise discrimination and seek to make both praise and blame equitable.

XII

Governors of provinces and rulers of districts must not levy double taxes upon the people. A country is not ruled by two sets of rulers, neither have the people two kings. The myriad people of the country are loyal to the king, the appointed officers of the government are also subjects of that same king. For what reason should they unjustly tax the people in the name of the government?

XIII

All those who occupy positions in the government should understand and attend to their duties. They may be absent because of sickness and for necessary travelling, but when present they should attend to their duties in a spirit of co-operation and not let them become complicated by their idleness.

XIV

All noblemen and their associates should be free from envy and jealousy. If you are jealous of another official, he may be jealous of you. The misfortunes that follow jealousy and envy are unlimited. Thus when another possesses superior wisdom you are not pleased, and when another possesses more skill you become jealous of him. If you have this spirit of envy and jealousy you will not meet a wise man in five hundred years, nor a saint in a thousand years. But how can a country be well ruled without wise men and saints.

XV

It has always been the law that a vassal should set aside his own affairs and obey the rulers. Generally when one thinks of his own affairs he becomes selfish and discontented and things do not turn out well. Then, if your affairs do not turn out well, they will certainly interfere with public affairs. If discontent and grudges arise they will disturb the public order. Therefore, as was stated in the first law, if the ruling body are harmonious, the people will become friendly with each other. This law is to be understood in the same spirit.

XVI

It was the spirit of the old law of public service, that men should be called upon only on suitable occasions. People should be called for public work during the cold winter weather, when they have leisure. They should not be summoned from spring to autumn when they must be busy farming and raising silkworms. How can they be expected to live if they are not permitted to attend to their farming and silkworms?

XVII

Do not decide important affairs on your individual judgment. You should discuss them with others. In small affairs this is not necessary, but when you are called upon to judge an important affair you must not make a mistake. If you discuss important affairs with others, your judgments will be sound and will be well received.

POSTSCRIPT

In answer to the wishes of our American friends, we have brought out a new edition of *The Teaching of Buddha* in English. Nothing gives us greater joy, for I think it is an important duty of all who believe in the teachings of the Buddha to have more people come in contact with Buddhism.

It was in 1934 that The Teaching of Buddha was published for the first time. It was done by the Federation of All Young Buddhist Associations of Japan. In order to commemorate their service, we have put the preface to the book in the first edition at the beginning of the book in this new edition.

Right after the first edition came out, Mr. Dwight Goddard, who took part in the work of translating the Scriptures, brought out an American edition of the same book in November, 1934. Twenty-eight years after, in 1962, we undertook the second edition of this book and printed 10,000 copies in the name of the Committee for the Celebration of the 70th Anniversary of the Introduction of Buddhism to America.

For this third edition, the Bukkyo Dendo Kyokai has undertaken the publication and printed 10,000 copies. I cannot help thanking the Buddha for having made us do this work.

Yehan NUMATA
Director, Bukkyo Dendo Kyokai.
President, Mitutoyo Mfg. Co. Ltd.

June, 1965

昭和四十年七月三十日　第三版印刷
昭和四十年八月十日　第三版発行

発行者　仏教伝道協会
　　　　株式会社三豊製作所内

寄贈者　株式会社　三豊製作所
　　　　社長　沼田恵範
　　　東京都港区芝田町五ノ三三ノ七号
　　　　　（徳栄ビル）
　　　電話東京(453)三三三二一番（大代表）